REAL LIFE

AN INSTALLATION

POETRY

Mead: An Epithalamion. University of Georgia Press, 2004.

Equivocal. Alice James Books, 2007.

Sarah—of Fragments and Lines. Coffee House Press, 2010.

100 Notes on Violence. Ahsahta Press, 2010.

RAG. Omnidawn, 2014.

Think Tank. Solid Objects, 2015.

PROSE

Surface Tension: Ruptural Time and the Poetics of Desire. Dalkey Archive Press, 2013.

Objects From A Borrowed Confession. Ahsahta Press, 2017.

Someone Shot My Book. University of Michigan Press, 2018.

TRANSLATION

Excess—The Factory. co-translated with Jennifer Pap, by Leslie Kaplan,
Commune Editions, 2018.

REAL LIFE

AN INSTALLATION

JULIE CARR

OMNIDAWN PUBLISHING
OAKLAND, CALIFORNIA
2018

Cover art:
Mona Hatoum, *Suspended*, 2011
High pressure laminate and metal chains
Dimensions variable
© Mona Hatoum. Courtesy White Cube (Photo: Hugo Glendinning)

Cover typeface: Avenir LT Std, Garamond 3 LT Std
Interior typeface: Copperplate Gothic Std, Garamond 3 LT Std

Cover & interior design by Cassandra Smith

Offset printed in the United States
by Thomson-Shore, Dexter, Michigan
On 55# Enviro Natural 100% Recycled 100% PCW
Acid Free Archival Quality FSC Certified Paper

Library of Congress Cataloging-in-Publication Data

Names: Carr, Julie, 1966- author.
Title: Real life : an installation / Julie Carr.
Description: Oakland, California : Omnidawn Publishing, 2018. | A collection
   of poetry and prose poems related to art installations mentioned in the book.
Identifiers: LCCN 2018015798 | ISBN 9781632430571 (pbk. : alk. paper)
Classification: LCC PS3603.A77425 A6 2018 | DDC 811/.6--dc23
LC record available at https://lccn.loc.gov/2018015798

Published by Omnidawn Publishing, Oakland, California
www.omnidawn.com (510) 237-5472 (800) 792-4957
10 9 8 7 6 5 4 3 2 1
ISBN: 978-1-63243-057-1

For Benjamin, Alice and Lucy

"Make art in conflict with real life."

Ralph Lemon

"This is where my real life is, the only life that's actually mine."

Reginald Shepherd

"Language has a plastic action upon the real."

Monique Wittig

FIRST MOVEMENT:
DYNAMIC INSTABILITY

MERE HEARTBEAT [9.5.11]

Lucy: That music on the radio, that's the Buddha's voice

Worse jobs report

Labor Day 2011 to Labor Day 2016

%

Tell me a witch story, she says.

Jerry and Lulu's Mom take them for haircuts. They have two moms? Should they? Yes. So one of their moms takes them for haircuts. Jerry gets his cut short and Lulu gets hers cut shorter. They watch in the mirrors as their hair falls to the floor. Suddenly, inside the mirror, the face of a very, very old woman. Dull yellow eyes. Sharp teeth in a gaping mouth.

She stares hard at Lulu as they walk out the door—

%

Job growth: 0

Interest Rate: 2

(What hid despair for a couple of days?)

The next day they get ready for a vacation. They pack hats, bathing suits, sunscreen, and head to the bus station. And there, in the bus station, the same old woman! Who? The one from inside the mirror. Glares and glares and will not stop. They climb onto the bus, she climbs on after, sits down near the driver.

The bus starts on its way. Old woman stands and waves her hands through the air, screeching magic words: *Envy no fictions! Punish no Rhymes!* Up the bus goes, into the sky—

%

I was "at a remove."
Is this "the foretaste of pain" or "an emptiness so sudden it leaves only the girders"?

Or it's just the candidate does not believe the right to privacy is part of the constitution. The candidate does not believe in contraception because he does not believe in sex without procreation (for women anyway). The candidate is second only to the other candidate.

The witch lands the bus on a cloud, tells all the people to get off, to watch the earth below. They see a boy searching for his dog; she turns that dog into a rat. Now he will never find it! A woman brushes her teeth; witch turns her toothbrush into a moth fluttering inside the woman's mouth. A baby cries for its bottle; she turns that bottle into a *fat worm*. But there is far more magic in her head than she can manage alone. *You* will help me, she screams at the people shivering on the cloud (clouds are cold)—

I walked downstairs, sat on the red chair, allowed the mix to "wash over me." Amassing yeasted minutes.

Said the candidate: "I believe that America is the one indispensable nation of the world."

O dispensable others—

%

Woke contrite, even ashamed, of growing so rapidly enraged as to throw the Apollinaire chapter with its big metal clip

    at his chest.
    He threw it back.

My gentle friend reassures me on the phone that all things will find their way to completion, that "Time is all that is wanted."

Chris: "Every battle has two sides, and so does poetry—
       The real and the ideal—"

Turns toward a man, trembling and meek. You! See that boy calling for his mother? Say these words: *Wonders drone and waters burn, call and call, milk-maker gone!* The man is afraid, but he speaks the words, too quietly at first, then louder and louder until he is screaming at the top of his lungs: *Wonders drone and waters burn, call and call, milk-maker gone!* The boy's mother: nothing but a broken rocking chair, leaning on its side. Now the witch turns to Lulu, but Lulu refuses, she refuses to say the words that will turn a baby's bottle into a worm, that will turn a man's arms into chains.

Bulging eyes, lipless frown, dripping nose, and raised her wand.

But Lulu is not afraid.

Grabs handfuls of cloud, throws them into the witch's face—

%

As tax cuts seen as best hope for jobs
As fires rage in Texas, California
As incarceration blooms data

The candidate proposes expansion of oil drilling, cutting of "discretionary" spending and "entitlements" (Medicaid, Medicare, Social Security, Housing Assistance, Head Start, SNAP).

The candidate proposes the end to all unions. A set back of all regulations. To cut corporate taxes to 15%.

Dark morning history page:

is there a process of absolution
there?

%

Every day I stroke the keys.

 Fires in Texas. Floods in Montana, Colorado, Iowa, North Dakota, Nebraska.

Throw it back.

AN IMAGE OF LOVE

As all in red, the candidates debate—their faces red, their podiums red, red as the red
wall behind—

it seems they debate
in an inferno.

*

The bus driver invites everyone back on the bus and, with some hesitation, some
doubt, drives shakily home through the sky

on this, the first cold evening of fall.

A book on "the feeling of being lived." A farewell to the mind / A farewell to the "scene" / An opening to the sky.

On the one hand, cut away all excess. On the other, welcome all things.

(A blank sleep. A heart slaked.)

Poverty at a 52-year high
15% of Americans
1 out of 6
46,000,000

And what is poverty?
In 2011 a family of four living on less than 22,000 a year, it says
Also called "absolute poverty"
(10,000 for an individual)
The median rent for a two-bedroom apartment in Denver in 2011: 14,400
In 2015, the "poverty threshold" for a family of four creeps up to 24,000
While rent for a two-bedroom rockets: 21,384
"This is truly a lost decade"
Today (it says): 27% of all blacks live in poverty, about the same for Hispanics
Today (it says): 17 million whites
Then there is "deep poverty," twice as bad as "absolute poverty"
"Poverty also swallowed more children" (1 out of every 4)

%

Darling American autoworker, darling American folk-music revival, dear American crowd, American bus stop, American American Merrill Lynch....

are you to blame?

Jerry and Lulu are playing cards by the fireplace, their parents reading in their chairs. Moms doze off, lights flicker. The fire grows bigger, hotter, brighter.

"Mom, Mom, the lights went out, wake up!" But their mothers cannot wake up. Why not? Just wait. Was it a witch? Just wait and see—

Asked if they favor more taxes for the rich, most will say yes.

The question remains: what do we mean by "more"? What do we mean by "rich"?

If a woman earns 399,000 she owes 117,000 to the government.

If she earns 400,000 she owes 140,000.

Most will say that's not fair.

The question remains: what do we mean by "that"? What do we mean by "fair"?

%

This work is missed.

This work is scum.

This work is bias.

My baby drinks tea.

My baby is a notorious gate.

A little sad.

A salty rod.

Sucked through to the other side of the fire, the children find themselves in a barren land. What's that? A land with no water, only fires burning here and there, and bits of burnt wood. What's burnt? You know, when you eat toast, how sometimes it has black parts? Yes. Burnt is the black part. Everything is like that, all the grass, all the trees. What did they drink? Nothing. No juice?

No juice or water. No milk? No milk.

What did they eat? Just coal, like the black parts of toast. It tasted terrible? Yes.

And now, I said to no one, I'll write a fourteen-line poem that includes one dream, one piece of news, one mention of the economy, one stolen line, and one imagined art installation. Like this:

1. A dark corner lit
2. The copies of trees
3. Not mine but a made place
4. The real renews itself each year
5. I'll do whatever the radios suggest
6. There lies the body; there lies the marvel
7. Faced with the extravagance of fruits
8. These woods are all woods
9. I am scuffed awake
10. How could I possibly join such urgency to such a quiet frame of mind?
11. The body announces nothing; it is itself the annunciation
12. Illustriously useless poetics
13. Then there is the hidden quality of genitals
14. Hurtling us even farther from the sun

"We are thirsty! We want to go home!" "We need something, anything, to drink!" The fire witch ignores them, walking around, stirring her fires, laughing her terrible laugh. Like what? Like this: "Ha, ha, ha, ha, ha, ha, ha!" Like this? "Ha, ha, ha, ha, ha!" Yes, just like that—

Jerry and Lulu begin to cry—

Salty tears. They lick them. But then Lulu: "Catch your tears in the cups of your hands! Throw them on the witch to diminish her magic!" What's that mean? Make her magic less powerful.

They hold their hands like little cups under their crying eyes, and the tears fall in—

*

Each time the fire witch draws closer to the children and laughs her terrible laugh, they cry harder.

"Now!" says Jerry.

*

Each time the witch comes near, laughing her terrible laugh, Jerry and Lulu cry harder, catch their tears in their cupped hands. Finally their hands are full!—

*

Paul Krugman likens the economic policies of our and European nations to "the bleeding cure."

*

"Now!" says Jerry.

A SHORT PROSE PIECE ON ONE OF THIS BOOK'S CENTRAL THEMES

We are raking leaves. Or I am raking leaves and she is wandering around picking up leaves, and a man shows up. He looks hot, I mean he looks overheated and sunburned or, the red face of an alcoholic, and I know when he calls me "ma'am" that he wants something. The usual "your neighbor told me to ask you," then shows his hand, the infected gash. I remember this from subways, the men with amputations exposed or diseased faces or wounded legs—he shows his hand and begins to speak. I'm standing still, not saying no not saying yes, I'm listening, and she walks toward him and holds out a leaf, which he takes, then she takes it back. He laughs a bit uncomfortably, and continues: the wife who left him, the kid at home, and how he had a Band-Aid but sweated it off, how he used to bring in two thousand a week, but now zero, and he lifts his hat to show the other wound, not so bad as the one on his hand, more a scrape or a bruise on the forehead, and then, almost in slow motion, still standing before him, she opens her arms and wraps them around his legs, her face too close to his crotch. I, also slow, say Lucy, come here, and he pats her on the back and says, aren't you affectionate. I take her hand and we go inside to find money, a ten is what I have, and I return and give it to him. Then he leaves, not without first offering to bring her his son's toys, since his wife left with his son. I say no, thank you, you don't know, he says, how awful this is to have to ask for work this way, and I say I'm sorry, and have a good day, which feels stupid. We are raking, there is silence, and I say, why did you hug him? I don't know, she says. I say, if Mommy and Daddy are not there, then don't hug a stranger, ok? but if we are and we say it's ok, it's ok. There is another silence. Then she says, don't ever say that again.

Farmer says his daughter in Afghanistan learned how to massage a heart to keep it pumping, to send a needle full of blood right into a collarbone to replace the blood pouring out of a wound. Double, triple amputees every day. What I wonder, he says, is who she will be when she comes

back home.

Corn in Iowa sold mostly overseas to feed cows in China, cows in Mexico. Very slowly we slide into the cloudy Denver dark.

For the sleeper slumped against the glass there is nothing to do about the runoff from synthetic fertilizer. Dear regulators,

please come back.

%

Was hoping to escape the bare language of fact.
But is it too late for complexities and games?

The yard holds its whiteness, witness, its

fallow-pleasures.

A city of dust, some radicals across the way. I want to know more about a slit and a hole. I enter into this circulatory system. Two boys remove their seatbelts to pummel one another. No shortening and no lessening. It follows that the goal of our economic system is the unhappiness of society. One grabs his mother's hair and yanks. How do we measure unhappiness? We find it in the breasts of women, which must be systematically lopped off like so much meat. I hope I have made you / very happy writes a daughter to her mother. A lamp reflected in a window is an adequate metaphor here. Is this normal, we ask a professional? No, this is not normal. But if nodes must return than nodes must return. Waking up every morning with a slight nausea. There's much I do not understand about the collapse of the financial sector. Suffer the living, but also the dead. I must apologize to my son and later to my daughters. We are trying to live in a house as if we were not the financial sector. As if we too were lopped off.

*

Is the exuberant use of unfamiliar words by one old man more valuable than the nursing of a newborn in the night?

"Tired of passing through the gloomy frame of history"

we try to locate our disgust in the present
as our pleasure.

BECAUSE I

saw the moon and then the moon she gone,
half moon sliding under protective oh—

and if *The New York Times* was the only news I ever saw I might feel
hopeful about protest movements and movies and underwear and prosthetics.

%

Some evangelicals believe in witches, demons, and "defensive shields." *That they
also believe in man-gods who return to earth has long been accepted.* Dear self, dear almost
finished life, to think with my jaw is not to think well.

Strikers in Oakland snow day my love a pillow floats into view give it up

The candidate accused of sexual harassment is the victim of a "witch hunt"

Coach can't afford the big house so we fuck a bit from behind

Lucy is proud super proud to do the twisty thing a celebration is in order, ice-cream!

A bit of blood on the pj's I made the lunches

Greece no confidence and possible severance from the zone French say

people before finance said let's go to dinner let's discuss our future but I bet you don't know a lot of interesting facts about the bush

baby. Remember when I was so depressed and now I am happy! and not "distant" but on top?

%

But I cannot remember what instigated this process—was it statistics, whether bad or good, or was it the longing for spiritual knowledge to emerge from inside the machine?

I am forbidden to understand. I speak into an empty space, no, into a "forest."

> "Are there real forests in this life?"
> "Yes, Lucy, there are real forests in this life."
> "Real ones? With bears and witches?"
> "Bears, yes, maybe not witches."

"Bears!?"

Silently, she reached out her long, thin, veiny hands.

A vast field strewn with rocks of all sizes.

Jerry, I think I know what to do!

*

She doesn't want us to play because she never played.
Maybe if we can trick her into playing, she'll let us go!

Great, said Jerry, let's make a house out of stones. When it's done, we'll ask her to play family.

*

Down on her hands and knees and meowed. *Here kitty, kitty, kitty.*

Pretend dinner made of rocks. Stretched just like a cat and meowed again.
Lulu went to "work," came back with more rocks, their "groceries." Scratched her head.

Said the witch: *I don't mind if you go home and play again, I don't mind if you have fun.*

But I don't want to stay here all by myself.

Girl in office crying because her boyfriend has a bad job in California and she has no job and poor health.

Girl in office crying because she graduates in two months and has no idea what to do next.

Boy in office crying because he went to the health center and was prescribed Adderall which "focuses thoughts and blocks distraction" but does not allow him to sleep for three nights and blocks, as well as distraction, the ability to write.

Boy in office crying because he cannot write the paper on the gay poet. The material, he says, "hits too close to home."

Girl in office crying because she has had a miscarriage.

Girl in office crying because she does not know grammar, never learned grammar, is graduating in one year without knowing what a sentence is.

%

Also, 23,000 homeless students in Colorado at this time.

A THING IS A HOLE IN A THING IT IS NOT

And so I should make some lists. Make a list of all the things I buy in a year and how much I paid for these things. Another of everything I didn't buy but wanted and could not afford. A third of all the things I didn't want but could have bought with the money I have—all the things and all their bags and all the things my body made. These investments that blossom or wilt. This debt that cowers in the cards. This social and compulsive spending on instant history. This constant and propulsive trading on floors. Cobalt streak in my daughter's hair: what price does it demand? This precise and brightening square on the wall. This easy and hopeless desire for factories. This refined and aggressive plan for tariffs. This inwardly observing mental discomfort, I should own up to its cost too. This alarming and elastic thrust toward isolation. This feeble and feral wish for protection, a protection that never can be bought. All the pains and all the pleasures—cheap ones like moistening the lips, expensive ones like raising a girl—these too should be written and priced. And on and on into a hole that swallows.

In 2013, 1 out of every 30 children in America is without a home
Statistics increasing in 31 states in the nation
2,483,539: an historic
high. Recall if you can—before the 1980s children were very rarely homeless

2010: 1.6 million
2013: 2.5
2017:

Colorado ranks 37th (50th being the worst) state in the nation for child homelessness

%

Ian says he's closing the soup kitchen. Can't afford anymore the security guard
Addicts and moms and veterans and teens chatting or with heads in arms

Think the phrase:

master bedroom

1. I sleep in the basement under more than one quilt; note the pens in their white cup and the beautiful speech of Hélène Cixous.

2. Dream a little boy walking toward me across a field.
3. Then off to the airport into deeper more northern parts and I don't like things I like words.

4. To think with the stomach is to not think well—my almost finished life is how I think of it—fingers on keys and the tired curves of my spine, wearing an ass.

My neighbor and I decide to create a commune made up of dancers, artists, and activists. But first we must train them. We gather them into a room and we begin a long, slow dance. The purpose of the dance is to teach people how to support one another and to be supported. Therefore, there's a lot of falling, catching, and lifting. When the dance is over I say, "Tomorrow's dance will be a lot more precise." What I have in mind involves touching one another's arms and hands—examining with all of our senses the split second between not touching and touching.

The kids and I are in someone else's apartment. The person who lives there is not home. We are looking through the rooms with urgency: opening drawers and cabinets, lifting objects from desks and countertops, staring at photographs, reading mail. We are, it seems, trying to find the person by examining all of their belongings. This is something we do regularly. It's a "practice." But in this case, since we ourselves once lived in this apartment, even as we are looking for the other person, we are also looking for ourselves underneath or within that person's things, underneath or within that person.

1. one burning lyric
2. stayed sayless
3. our technique's so feline
4. it takes its time
5. like a trail of ants
6. across a hall
7. nothing's not
8. born
9. a primate a psyche
10. an umbrage a rag
11. say God in the
12. beaten air's
13. birds we'll eventually
14. be

*

My desires, as a person perhaps beyond the "middle of my life," are to remember to feel the lived-in body and to allow my children to leave me (primary).

To contribute to a revision of fairness, to be blunt, to speak. Further, to allow my parents to leave me (secondary).

One girl responds to the urban camping ban by painting cartoon eyeballs onto the sides of buildings / where she used to sleep.

Opponent to the Right to Rest Act (Denver, April 27, 2015):
"We don't support criminalizing the status of homelessness, just the behavior."

%

To eat. To "buy a garden bench" [says Lucy: "vench"]
The yard holds its whiteness, witness, fallow pleasures.

2 REAL LIFE ARRANGEMENTS

1.

The Pope's gentle fix in the erect election, his slacked calm—

Complains about his job

2.

Just as historical depth resides in the folk-art commodities of the 1970s

Celan's death, that lovely face, sits in the incremental creases

of the sky or a guy's eye, in the pigeon-coated
improvisational dusk

On July 24, stars fell down wells, becoming an owl's jewely eyes.

On August 6, the poet put his penis on the tumblr page.

Wind / leaves / wind / leaves / wind / lives / leave / delve / in wind

The word "blown" cannot mean much to a child, but everything always ends up
      otherwise, O beautiful stranger.

Remember how you said you were dreaming about a bee and then you woke up, and when
      you closed your eyes again, the bee was gone?

The sun, an engrossing inglorious pulp. The abstracted buildings, stitched up by
      sleep.

This drink is strange, making itself known

in our throats.

B and I read *The Odyssey* out loud. It takes a long time to meet the hero, and when we finally do, he's crying by the shore. Sobs long before he speaks. There's a lot of crying in *The Odyssey*. There is also much eating. They eat, always, before they talk. First feed the stranger, then ask him who he is. Maybe there's a connection between crying and feeding strangers. Between not feeding strangers and *not, any longer, crying.*

*

Elana's house underwater. Jessica's house underwater. Sidney's apartment underwater. Elana's job insecure. Margaret's job insecure. Julia has no job. Ian has no job. Delia seeks a new career (cafeteria manager). Teresa seeks a new career (speech therapist). Greg loses his job. Erika, food stamps to supplement her job. Graham wants a better job. Keera has no job. John drinks his job. Ella gone. Now John gone. Brooke can't work. Don not promoted. Sasha no clients.

Seated on the shore, gazing out into the "barren ocean," crying. Saying not a word.

Also recall if you are able that in the two thousandth and fourteenth year of our lord, also the Hebrew year of 5775 and the Islamic year of 1436, a man in the ninth decade of his life on earth, residing in the State of Florida, formerly the Spanish colony La Florida, and prior to that the land of the Seminole, was three times cuffed and three times taken down and three times fined for feeding chicken and cheesy potatoes to strangers with no steady home.

*

The children are damaged inside a reality show about cakes and I've got one house and 1 in every 31 adults under some form of correctional supervision. 1 in 6 black men at some time in some place.

An evolving statistic I can see in only one way: The Internet.

The phrase: *thrown around in the world*

ENDEAVORS NOT REWARDED

And now I address even you, my friend, with growing hostility
while gazing into the face of the opposition with the soulless eyes of the filmed.

I carry no cash, so have no cash to give.

Did I tell you how much I love reading *The Odyssey* with you?
(In the car) (Silent high five)

The suitors are evil, says B, and they *know* they're evil

The candidate runs for the little man
The candidate welcomes articles from a psychoanalytic perspective
The candidate's music is full of gentle dark soundscape, an "overflowing sink"
The candidate features Jonas, who believes his father to have been murdered
"The Candidate sat fingering his testicles through the crotch of his velour
       track-pants"
"Why would you want to kill your baby," the candidate asks
Answer the following questions to see which candidate is most like you
"He's a photographer, let him take my picture!" exclaims the candidate
The candidate is an installation artist
The candidate's comeback surprises even himself
Of the candidate: "He's so irrelevant, his speech is just brackets for sale"
Is God too just brackets around earth?

Repetition, which is the business of psychosis, organizes the drama before me

Early sun sharpens the outlines of trees

Sweat under sweater   wheels ribbon the road
I hear the birds cawing   because of the sun   that ancient sound

"Sickness is furious   in mothers and   daughters"

And because I wish to assume control of *my own death*:

Tim, I am sorry

NOSTALGIA FOR THE INFINITE (DE CHIRICO)

Whatever was lifted whatever plundered
is now submerged in bursts of song
The devil laughs in slow motion as a girl delivers flowers by the armful

*

"Dear ones," says Reverend Foster at Rufus's funeral in my mother's copy
of Baldwin's *Another Country*, "don't lose heart. Don't let it make you bitter.
Try to understand. Try to understand. The world's already bitter enough, we
got to try to be better than the world."

*

One window with teeth
Which way is the door?
Felt my all inside questioning running through there

END FIRST MOVEMENT

INTERLUDE: A REAL LIFE FICTION

Today I am told that the four-year-old has excellent powers of concentration. She also does not know that if others cut her in line, she can tell them to stop. Her teacher instructs her to say, "I am first!" for we are a nation of firsts; her brain instructs her to let the others go ahead and not to interrupt when others are speaking (even if she is thirsty). Her brain also instructs her to ask my opinion before she makes a decision, such as which candy to have or what shirt to wear.

I accept this. I no longer say, "It's up to you!" Instead I offer an opinion and she considers this as she makes her choice. She is inclined, then, to "think about others," to "think *with* others" as well. These were not things we necessarily emphasized.

In the morning of the day she was born I watched the sunrise over the mountains while birds whipped past the window. Except for one theatrical moment ("I don't know who I am!" I cried out from the bathtub—a false statement I thought might help me), her birth was a peaceful event. The pregnancy too was peaceful; though I slept badly, I listened to the night-sounds of Boston or Denver.

The other daughter practices a more complex economy. Capable of reasoning out the motives (especially the ugly ones) of all people, she's gifted with insight. And yet, her sense of entitlement when she was little was, if anything, somewhat exaggerated. Hosting a party, she'd insist on having the most and on being first ("It's *my* party," she'd say). She was also hyper-aware of all criticisms levied her way, and at four claimed, "no one likes me." As you might expect, arguments with friends were frequent. And yet, within this tumult, she was and is powerfully assured, excelling in things physical and academic. And singing. I will say, then, that I have always considered her fiery disposition to be directly connected to the conditions of my pregnancy and her birth. Which were not particularly peaceful.

%

One cannot tell the story of a pregnancy without first speaking of sex. But it's exactly sex that I don't want to speak of. In one model, sex is the "power that tears experience from ordinariness," in another, it's the "founding of a being-in-common."

There was, at any rate, a dream from which I woke with an intense feeling of shame, rekindled by the face of any man I encountered that day and for the two or three days after, during which we were staying in a commercial campground in Key West, celebrating the dawn of a new century among the flamingos, the pelicans, and the pink T-shirts and faces of Floridians and tourists alike. It was sunset, and I was pregnant, but not with either of the daughters I now have. I was pregnant with a non-one, a person who had already removed itself from the scene of new modesty and soon to be destroyed Pax Americana into which we wheeled our then two-year-old son. This non-one had already died, and I wore my hair in braids, as if to say, "No problem! I'm nothing but a girl!" while the dream followed me with its charcoal sketches flung under a bed, its dim windows, the one arm circling. I won't describe further, but I will say it hinted at "a new form of dividing up the common world." I was pregnant and the baby inside me was dead. I was married and had dreamed of a man who, like the baby, did not exist.

But all stories of the body ought to begin much earlier. There was the time I stood from my chair and walked directly into a wall.

%

After the death of the youngest one's friend, a five-year-old boy named Destin Self, she tells me she now knows that the dead do not float up into the sky. "No?" I say. "No," she answers, "they just turn away from the other persons." The non-one inside me had truly "turned away from the other persons." As we drove past a strip mall in Northern Florida—a Chinese restaurant, a dollar store, a yoga place—I felt it die. I was no longer nauseous. No longer anything. I wore my hair in braids.

Was this, the family I was making, nourished by the embodiment of its own idea? I don't know. But I can tell you this: during a period of ten years, I was pregnant five times. When added together, these pregnancies occupy a full three of those ten years. The nursing that followed three of those five pregnancies filled seven and a half of those ten years.

That which did not exist had to be made manifest. This was the message my body imparted. "This opposition between death and life was too simple."

%

That night, we left the piers just minutes before the fireworks began. Our son had long since fallen asleep in his stroller. I no longer cared about the new millennium, the "post-modern rupture." Anyway, it was already a new millennium in Europe; we'd watched the Eiffel Tower swing lights from its points like jump ropes held at one end by angels.

Pauline Pfeiffer Hemingway, despite being, by some accounts, an absent mother, had a birthing chair in her bedroom. This I had examined closely on the last day of the old millennium when visiting the Hemingway House. I thought about this chair later when squatting on the bed, rocking on all fours, or sitting with no dignity whatsoever on the toilet, trying to give birth to a baby that was someone. The birthing chair was made of a dark smooth wood with handles on the sides and a C shaped opening through which the baby could fall.

In 1927 Pauline Pfeiffer Hemingway had the greatest haircut and was the assistant editor of *Paris Vogue*. Earnest was dapper. In a rage, he threw her into the pool, the pool I circled, gazing into its murky surface, looking, one could say, for her face.

To go no further forward, I tend my telling back.

The man who lived in our basement apartment was gentle but jumpy on coke and racked by guilt, for I was not even sixteen. Later, he chose a red-haired woman more his age. I saw that she was suitable and despised her. And so, with my boyfriend in my upstairs bedroom, I amplified my cries so basement dwellers might hear them. I was not yet sixteen and wore a plaid kilt with a slit. You are my sunshine, he said. A girl's slit emits no light. Mothers go to work and rage at the sink in the evenings.

I was the second child of a woman raised to be married, still beloved among us despite her ghostly something-like life. No further "music classes" or "art projects" entertain her, though she was a knitter, a weaver, an embroiderer, a seamstress, a paper-doll maker, a cook, a baker, a gardener, a protester, and a lawyer. Upholder of justice, she "raged at the sink."

A "type abject and vicious," and at the same time deeply nourishing, though short.

%

During a period of fifteen years, my mother was pregnant six times by two different men. These pregnancies, added together, lasted forty-five months. The nursing increased her time of being "not one" by only an additional year (I estimate). A "hot tempered, bold…impatient woman," and in trees often, I gazed down.

There was an earlier pregnancy, the first, confirmed over an airport payphone, which lead me to sit, slumped against the wall in the airport bathroom, crying. I boarded the plane and heaven sent me a woman. She did not know me, or know my trouble, but she allowed me to sleep against her shoulder, the sleep of the deeply distraught, of the wounded. Why would I say wounded? Pregnancy could be seen this way—as an injury—for this was not a baby, because a baby I would not keep. My nipples ached in the swimming pool. And though I was pregnant, I snorted coke with my boyfriend when his parents had gone to work, for this was not a baby, for not a baby I would keep. (But to trace her age in the air now, she is 27, and beautiful.)

I slept on the woman's shoulder clothed in brownish tweed. She stroked my hair (to speak figuratively). The Berkeley hills were never so chilly, sunset never so garish. I slept.

I had not yet imagined the cauliflower as a form of a family, but rather saw myself as a "witness to an inassimilable strangeness," or as one whose fate, as Fitzgerald put it, would pull me across from nothing to nothing.

There was within me a sentimentality that pushed: at last, I wanted to read the Bible. The nothingness that has neither space nor time is ready to "pop," say physicists, into "something" at any moment.

A room of yellow and kitsch in a country house. It made me feel worthy to pray. It made me feel Christian. And old.

%

I delivered my news (pregnancy #5) to a homemade kitchen table beneath two windows of blue glass. This was something. Something weighty and something of a relief for it "put the nail in the coffin" of all my prior sins.

%

At fifteen a single muscle ran from the center of my face to the space between my legs, a single taut muscle like a monochord.

Earlier (at 12), I excused myself at the theater. That stepfather (not my own) reached his hand out to stroke my ass as I scooched past his knees. Another ass-stroker was my college professor who invited me into his apartment, "door's open!" from within the shower, bathroom door ajar. I found something to read in the living room. Wife not home. Son at school. He comes out of the bathroom with the towel around his waist and stands there. I say and do nothing and eventually he retreats for clothes. But the biggest (though shortest) ass-stroker was my sister's babysitter, basement dwelling aspiring actor whose hand went up my skirt all summer long.

All of these tales now bring to mind the art of Thornton Dial, the baby dolls and flowers shellacked and painted sickly yellow, the straws, wires, bits of chain-link painted the colors of battle. For battle there was when at 20 in a hotel bedroom I discovered a stranger who, having crawled through the open window, now pressed his entire body on top of my own, one hand firm across my mouth, the other yanking sheets. A moment so ordinary it simply enters the atmosphere as a gas.

A gas that floats and keeps on floating until it reaches the "top" overhead, the sky-not-sky, the enclosure I once thought an aperture. And there, steadily, it remains.

END INTERLUDE 1

SECOND MOVEMENT:
THAT WHICH IS ONLY WHAT IT IS AND NO MORE THAN THAT

Let's see where the voice goes today (throaty murmur of a dove):

Pressing my fingers to my chest, I slept exhausted. My two little girls with their movies on, and I knew the boy was really dead, and the other one, by her own hand. All could not *be* "well."

       A damaged nerve can now be chemically patched.
       Can they fix the nerves in my head?

*

       "Here I am!" exclaimed my demented mother to a group of people, total strangers, with whom she hoped

she might belong.

*

Therefore, in response to the request for more information about my daughters' health histories I can say only this:

> Undecidable content: the majesty of the well. The problem-trucks took fear off-site. Angels of consumption, what difference do fingernails pressed against periphrastic gravestones make? My goddess is called "god's nightly shadow." No, there is no "history."

In real life it takes a long time to remember what month it is. To accept what we are together. Um, um. Tim scratches.

This rhythm is historical, gestural, political, responsive, continuous, and of a specific body.

Language is inseparable from shit, is a mode of wide expression.

*

The sob initiates as a very quiet pressure just behind the nose.
Faces confirm one another.

Through a debilitating head thing I see
the candidate signing a Personhood Pledge in order to define life at the moment of
fertilization

"The younger the girl the better!" proclaims the Subway mogul

%

"The back of the head waits for death," I read, reaching back to touch mine

26,000 sexual assaults in the military in one
single year

Jeffrey Krusinski, placed in charge of the sexual assault prevention and response unit
for the Air Force is himself arrested for sexual

battery: 238
convicted

(fractured sense of time/teeth/justice)

%

When women find themselves stationed between doodle, cartoon, and gag, sleeping on the couch again, vague and injured, can't labor no more in the video stream.

The phrase: *Thrown around in the world*
The sentence: *Don't ever say that again*

It now becomes imperative to talk about depression and its sources. I am no expert. My friend says it's like having trees growing out of your feet. No, he said something more interesting than that, but one of the symptoms of depression is that you can't remember stuff. I thought, maybe it's just the weather. I don't like the coming heat and I don't like the season in which my mother was, I could say, "incarcerated" in her own body. Which is perhaps one way to define depression.

A fugitive ran from country to country. The newscasters spat at him. My friend called this "The death of liberalism, one pundit at a time."

I wondered about ambition and then I didn't. It was a come-and-go concern.

THE QUOTIDIAN RAISED TO THE LEVEL OF THE ATMOSPHERIC

"I've only ever wanted to experience my life," Alyosha Karamazov, laying the Elder down, whispers into his flushed face

The eye is "tarnished"
Yet I've only ever wanted to see

*

Dear Sisters,

In *Brothers K*, the mute girl gives birth to a boy in a garden shed. Her rapist is not punished, but laughed at for fucking a mute

To reproduce is a human right, is a "ring of fire" into which a woman moves
in order to temporarily escape herself,
to "feed on her own extinction"—it says

*

"The fields
are
lethal
but pretty in Autumn"

(Such economical moods are only possible in poetry)

"I dreamed I was in a forest that was burning down around me and I couldn't get out. The next night I dreamed my legs were made of wood."

Ben, 15 years old: Elgar Cello Concerto and *The Autobiography of Malcolm X*

in his head.

*

In this, the next "stage of life," I will be both angrier and more compassionate. It's a guess. I have no fucking idea.

Bread dough, which I knead, smells exactly like my husband's body.

Lavinia (also murdered), Lucrece (death by suicide). Threatened: Isabella, Marina, Miranda, Silvia, some say, Juliet

Also, my students: A, M, and S (in one semester)
also N's daughter

%

Men rape women all the time, said my 12-year-old daughter. When the book goes, "they beat her up," it means they raped her, it just didn't want to say it, she says.

The phrase: *Pre-traumatic stress syndrome*

(My all inside questioning running through there)

1. It has to begin somewhere
2. She harass with enjoyment
3. Tired of the topic before I
4. Start. Cause if she's not raped
5. She's the criminal killing the
6. Thing. So rape her to
7. Save her from herself. O
8. Lovely
9. Flaky, she'll be data or she'll be
10. Tagged
11. So she made herself a border and hung there
12. Pregnant or bleeding or pregnant and bleeding
13. Been full a long time with
14. Time and the gray clouds streaming in

(Daughter: because I loved you boldly and got you out into something breathable, I made an installation and called it *fucked*.)

We sat side by side at the counter, reading the poems out loud.

I got up to peel a squash.

In the other room: horses arranged in a stable, piano lesson, "homework."

I tried to approach a naïve awareness of the earth and my place on it.

"My 6 months of military training did not let me see the world in a more positive light," said someone.

        The stink of the real lay like a scum on the pages of the poems.

*

The best part of each day was the end of that day suggested I would not be afraid to die.

1. a saw hung in our garage
2. the executioner's cloak in his
3. the world as we reach for it, recedes
4. I have since attempted to fill this lacuna

A FOURTEEN-LINE POEM ON THE WISH TO TOUCH ANOTHER PERSON'S FACE

1. of course this is to move all too quickly
2. we have tested, worn out, and disfigured various versions of "the person"
3. is my spine "bad"?
4. we have finally done away with the desire to be seen at a picnic
5. no we haven't
6. I forgot to put my hand on the tree's bark
7. but stretched beneath the branches, I let the pollen
8. fall into my eyes
9. at midnight I was alone
10. not everything is touched by light
11. a font too small to read in a book titled *Insights*
12. you and I and the blue world in a crimson flower
13. it's not a flower, it's a bone
14. with no clear beginning or end

One considers a great sprawling work that refuses to keep anything out
One considers our candidate with his uncountable riches (women, send me your works!)
One considers the "poverty paradigm," the deepening divide, the 40,000,000
destitute here at "home"
0 my mental season, the tulip absorbs the snow into its bulb

*

The human understanding is not a dry light, but is infused with desires and affections
(Francis Bacon paraphrase)

To see a fine substance strangely: forms of life, come in

The thing you have to know about the tree-witch is that she can turn herself into a golden bird with wide wings and a long orange beak flitting around in the aviary.

*

Even a witch in the form of a bird will melt if she cries.

How do the children make her cry?
    She becomes nothing but a golden pool on the ground.

The hungry tiger bit her leg. She cried from pain, not disappointment (as is usual).

*

The tree-witch in the form of a golden bird wants nothing more than to capture and enslave all the other birds in the aviary. Needs one feather from each of the other birds for the enslavement potion.

J and L, in order to save themselves, must gather these feathers one by one.

"Sadness lingers," says Charles Blow after the Martin case has closed (7.2013). "A life you take latches on to you."

*

"I was nothing and I slept," Ivan confesses to Alyosha, a confession I have read three times, on three separate nights, just before dropping into sleep.

> *I am nothing.* But still in that
> *I wanted to be loved.*

Girls in their sudden beauty standing at chain link are invited
into his car. They take
three steps back and then
they run. No one
can be arrested for speaking
to girls. Three steps back
then run. The man
with the cut on his hand
the cut that since October
has not healed (he reopens it?) asks
my baby again
for change. Nothing
wrong with asking.
No crime.

1. immobility is the source of their perfection
2. yanked the toaster cord out of the socket
3. because the car would not start
4. we walked home singing
5. I have become "for you"
6. for if I claim never to have loved you
7. I will lose the part of myself that misses you
8. and so will miss that part of myself
9. at 3:30 in the morning and at 7
10. I don't like my face anymore
11. than I like this tender, fragile, pink balloon
12. I wear the jeans you wore though they are torn everywhere
13. for without these jeans covering only just my crotch
14. how will I ever feel you?

In the dream the baby boy was nursing. He wanted to nurse because it was sexy, and I was ok with that. But we had to *pretend* it was for nourishment so the others would not be shocked or consider the nursing a kind of violence.

This is the central confusion of real life:

The body as erotic object, the body as food, the body as hunger, the body as victim, the body as perpetrator.

The solitary person turns on the television and waits. The room is dedicated to her. It is her "hotel." She lies down on the bed. No dust. Windows do not open. Through the floor, a treadmill's rhythmic whine.

On the walls, photographs of people whose curved backs, whose exhausted flesh, need chemicals daily or hourly. Sheets of charred wallpaper hang from the ceiling and curl.

You are invited. You wander around looking for yourself among the photographs. Eventually you join the woman on the bed. If you sleep, you will dream of her hands on your face.

*

"What does beautiful mean?"
"You. You are beautiful."
"No. What does the *word* beautiful really *mean*?" etc.

END SECOND MOVEMENT

INTERLUDE: 10 DERIVATIVES

1. *All that is Solid (or what I know about the body)*

Fluid sits in the ear, waiting for sound. The nervous system holds memories of pain and pleasure for an entire lifetime. Tightness in the palate or tongue causes corresponding tightness in the pelvic floor and cervix. The diaphragm flutters. The earliest movement is the movement of a starfish. Eyes dart upward. Lungs rise on a diagonal plane (one of the few diagonals in the body). Touch stimulates brain growth. Oxytocin fires in bursts. If touched, wounds heal faster. An aura of Mother-Mary-Blue shines above the head. Middle finger is connected to liver. Something beats in the back of the skull. Hormone, from the Greek "impetus," or "onset," or "rush." The "onset of darkness" secreted by the brain is affected not only by the time of day, but also by the season. Blue light suppresses sleep. Depression lodges between vertebrae. Fear in the muscles of the head. Over time, the feet lose sensation. Fat lives in the eyes. Just before death, feet and hands empurple. Desire is imaginary. Beginning we are two, concluding, we are one. Teeth go first, last longest. A chip in a bone will not heal. The brain will be lost, becoming only an ambient teleology.

2. *So Will You*

enter the lyrical stream?—socialism returns to France—Wisconsin's girls get pregnant at 19, 20, 21—is someone crying upstairs?—the news suggests a shift from austerity—toward what lycanthropic dream?—the whistling of my son—how do the markets respond?—Debaters sell soot—behind a revolving door—but the bank is un-enterable—like a bag in a bag—a plane in the sky—a body asleep in the arms of its mother—a glass of vodka—tattooed to her arm—so will you—wander a house—in the early morning—light—

3. A Dandelion

And even if the candidate did not snip the locks off the blond boy's head, he did sign on to the Ryan plan. My response is to let my plant die, an austerity measure. I was just enacting this response while shopping in my head. But to really get the thing, I'll need to first buy gas. Luckily, ExxonMobil loves me and loves all my children, especially when I flush the toilet, which I do about nine times a day. ExxonMobil and I both love flowers. And we have earnings in the 9.5 billion per quarter. Here's what CEO Rex W. Tillerson and I have to say: I am a woman and I write in opposition to the subject/object split. I prefer to consider myself multiple. I am very excited to be drilling in the arctic. I love my red chair from which I rarely rise. I make the same as the president of the Ohio University system, and that's just over 2 million a year. With a dandelion in my shirt pocket, I am on the living list of living people where I reside.

4. News and Ontology

Give space (since life ends unawares)
To hale a coffined corpse adown the stairs;
For you will die (Thomas Hardy condensed)

5. *Horse in a Truck*

My favorite part was when they laughed and laughed
That was my favorite part too
And the horses
Yeah

6. *Vibratory Nation Poem*

Once I read what the climate change deniers had to say, I felt so happy for one
hour. Like in the days before my mother got sick.

7. *Capital/Capitol*

Make a leaf
Make clouds
Make a layer of gas that blocks the sun

Make leaves and give one to everyone—Stir the ocean—Stir the ocean to bring
up the deep cold—Enter a flower—Stay married—Only adopt. Adopt adopt—
Use no wood (back to ideas)—There are people then there are—The People—
Stand in line and preorder—Preorder the hats—Hold out your wrists—(they'll
beat you anyway)—The river gave birth to you—Now give birth to the river—
Close your mouth—Close both your mouths—Dissolve in the origin—The
clarion sun—Attach trees to the floor—Cut the strings—Play—

8. *Clouds Doing Nothing*

After forty-nine bodies with heads, hands and feet severed have been cleared
from the desert town of San Juan, children can once again frolic and couples
can once again hold hands (but not men) while the girdle makes a comeback in
Queens: "We still need to live while they do what they do."

9. *Musical Notation*

Genentech will manufacture Crenezumab, designed to attack amyloid plaques

And if "irritability, sadness, crying, and anxiety" are Cardinal Features of The Disease,
who's to say I do not already have it?

The sun has risen on a Wednesday
The Ryan Plan hopes to reduce government spending to .3 percent of GDP (except
military). All trees "leafed out"

While Walmart will build over the graves of slaves (not metaphorically)
a Floridian mother of four (33) shoots and kills them all

10. *Grotesque*

The body is its own conclusion

Thumb-sized bird in a leafless tree with yellow flowers
A pool with nobody in it

The ability to hear (the shots) is dimensionless
We cannot stop

hearing them

END INTERLUDE 2

THIRD MOVEMENT:
LIFE REARRANGED

A man murders another man who is having sex with the first man's wife. The murderer is exonerated because of the law that allows for killing if one feels oneself to be threatened or assaulted.

In what way is a man having sex with a woman threatening or assaulting that woman's husband? In a way that thinks of the woman as an extension of her husband's body. Make love to my wife, says this law, and you are raping me.

%

gotta get over before we go under
gotta get under before we go over

raise our food like the man

get sexy sexy
people people

WISDOM COMES ONLY FROM INVESTIGATING MOTHER

As the earth warms we can access the oil in the arctic!
Home again home again jiggety-jig
To London to London to buy a fat hog

Mr. Hernandez returned voluntarily to New York and led investigators
to the address where he had worked, described to them what he had done

Pussy cat pussy cat where have you been?
33 years prior he'd murdered a seven-year-old boy
The story omits any motive

Later, we discover his confession to be fabricated
He and the boy's death: return to obscurity

In pain or in pregnancy the body makes itself known.

Says the candidate:

"It has been my experience that when dealing with females, you need to treat them as though they have a mental disorder."

No, he didn't say that. But the common space creates it and we, in our hunger, repeat.

Are we "haunted by the imaginary as an irresistible supplement"? Or are we simply

masochistic?

A FOURTEEN-LINE POEM ON THE MYTH OF HAPPINESS

1. Some months are like dogs

2. The heart beats faster

3. I have written no novel

4. The beginner, and only the beginner

5. Guarantees political freedom

6. Some months race rats

7. If sound is of a shattered body

8. One of thousands

9. Since the wars began

10. What is that that

11. I privately catalogue

12. A family fortress?

13. The future-time

14. Of skin?

Workers at Walmart (1.8 million): 8.58/hour
The CEO of Walmart (1): 11,000/

hour

36,000,000 dollars spent

every hour of
every day

at Walmart

1. Time is thought of as the movement toward the
2. other person. The
3. absolutely other.
4. Like the woman on the plane
5. who yanked the head off a chicken
6. pulled fifty bucks from its insides
7. then stuffed the dead chicken into a bag
8. and threw it away.
9. If insatiable desires describe us
10. never do we escape the boundaries of the self.
11. She was arrested, right there on the plane
12. for having placed a dead bird in the trash
13. and not for the fifty bucks
14. which she had stolen.

%

"Treat money like an art material, otherwise it's going to fuck the art," said Damien Hirst standing beside his diamond skull—

(Or, you could have given it all away)

(Understatement is not a political tactic)

THE ACCIDENT OF BIRTH

Black man in a black suit on the Tube reads a black book titled *On Being Black*.
White woman beside him writes furiously on white paper.

Is the self the reason "we ascribe belatedly to a sequence of effects"? Or is the light
reflected in the dark morning window

someone missing someone young?

PESSIMISM OF THE MIND, OPTIMISM OF THE WILL

This duplicity of our being:

white went for one, color for another

White prays

smashes an eye that blinks

(We are done being white said the party)

This morning, as the sun stays more or less still and we revolve, all 300,000,000 of us, or those who look at things on screens, are gazing on the faces of five men, gray or balding, earners of at least ½ a million a year, each of whom knew that one in their group was raping boys in showers and not one of whom said so. Also, he forced them to suck him, and he masturbated on them.

I, just like you, allow no limits on my looking. Because I am free, beautifully free, I look at everything they give me to look at.

And into my freedom I inflict
the punishment of brute
fact.

1. So stripped of plans I had to lie down and cry

2. Or begin again with methods and strategies refined

3. I loved all my teachers, one by one, until, one by one, they all died

4. I used the six of spades as a bookmark, just where the author admits to incest

5. We were in the psychodrama of nonviolence training

6. When we walked into the sea, hand in hand, the cops followed us

7. Seawater flowing into their guns

8. Now a cloudy morning, just where the author asserts his commitment to the self

9. For a long time it seemed the self was anathema

10. But after surveillance had its way with us, we had to return the individual to the scene

11. In order to adore her, her nipples and her cunt, and also her eyes

12. The boats of the past bore her as their figureheads; those on deck, protected by her presence

13. This was "the bad neighborhood of real life" in which the female body wore its insides on the outside

14. That was how we wanted her, wasn't it?

I took a baby from the river
I swung upon a gate
I carried my weapon when I went to market
A fly lived nastily
Until damaged

*

Written in the dust:

    "Master—

    Make me a city
       — Visitor"

*

"A world transformed to accommodate infinite desire would be a world of magic."
(But the witches have left us now.)

A dirt floor, the walls of a cage laid flat under the rooting light of the sun. A girl's face and torso projected onto the far wall.

You want to enter this room without touching anything. But this is impossible. *Your presence, most of all, a discharge.*

The girl's hand-motions imitate precisely the hand-motions of the President giving a speech about the war, though in fact, she's only describing the activities of her mother in the bathroom.

*

The room is dirty. You want it dirty. The walls are smudged. You like them that way.

Her eyes blink. Her eyes are unbearably clear. Is she the "victim" of this room or its presiding angel?

No door through which to enter, no door through which to leave.
No visible light source, but there is light. It comes from everywhere.

A body is sleeping on a platform, a white cloth over its face. It's unclear whether male or female, impossible to know race, age, whether sick or well. Rise and fall of the chest, a slight flutter at the edge of the cloth.

In an adjacent room sits anyone's father, an old man. You can enter this room from one of six doors. No matter by which door you choose to enter, you will confront only his back. No matter by which door you leave. From the angle of his head and the slight lift of his shoulders you can tell that he is listening to you as you come and go.

The installation artist is an "orthopedist who makes artificial limbs for parts of your body that you don't even know you've lost."

The installation artist "aims to induce doubt about the very structure of what we take to be reality."

The installation artist "puts something sweet in someone's mouth—and that is very sexy."

*

But now let us turn to the cows, sold at record rates months ahead of schedule. Prairies are scorched dirt. Not even a cow can eat scorched dirt. Goodbye cows. The ranchers are "just sitting here crying." Without water, the corn is glutted with nitrogen and grows toxic. Without rain, irrigation ponds bloom algae. Cows' milk runs dry and calves starve. "It's hard. But it's called life," says Ms. Manning whose family's been in the business of raising cattle to slaughter for 200 years.

On this day, just after the very moment when the movie could have been said to have
begun, Ashley, age 6, who had been kept up late

and taken to the movies,
for there was no babysitter,

was, at the very moment when the movie could have been said to have begun,
shot dead.

One other one was my student's student. Another, B's friend.

I cried all the way to the JCC until Lucy told me to stop.
"Breathe for those who cannot breathe," said someone into the airwaves.

My mother in her bed, after the loss of all language, will still whisper

"psss, psss, pisss"

%

"Does a fly have memory?"

It's so close, the death of 12 in a movie theater—we breathe it in.
What

do we breathe out?

%

Ben slowly halves an apple.
That could be, if I let it, a kind of purity.
If I let it.
If I were to be
so afraid.

MUTED BURDEN

Just like Andrea Zittel I wanted to make something from nothing, to fill the empty vault of a national cry.

*

I like America and America likes me (says Joseph Beuys).
Loads a body into an ambulance. Turns on the siren.

Going home so often means going *down*.

Drought in the heartland, death in the multiplex. Rough in the heart landed death in the multiple. Rough tin the heat landed death in them

Doubt in that hot man heat in thee—

A FOURTEEN-LINE POEM ON THE HOLE AT THE CENTER OF THE COUNTRY

1. the gap opens the wound
2. unidentified youth jump across
3. "the lying-line"
4. a self-like self
5. with "spurious" emotions
6. is here now in these lines held hostage
7. (the plagiarized bits are often not exact)
8. this bird distorts
9. and misuses
10. but now I must turn to the real
11. life business of love
12. the porch at night: dark with laughter
13. and a dirge-like song
14. for you, just for you

*

A stream is a tiara for a god
or more like a child eating scabs?

THE CODEPENDENCY OF MOURNING AND HOPE

Tomorrow at Infinity Park ammunitions manufacturer Magpul will be giving away 30-round magazines to the first 1,500 people who show up. All you have to be is 18 to get one. "That sort of thing never happens here," says the neighbor of the two dead little boys. Yes it does.

The phrase

semblance shattered

A FOURTEEN-LINE POEM ON INFINITY PARK

1. We are coping with a huge set of historical data
2. Understand, the 5,400 deaths are really 16,000
3. So many uncountable
4. In the house of the human body
5. Gauzy curtains creamy walls
6. A perfect circle of dead grass where once was a fire
7. You, leaning back in your chair
8. "Yes, I want to love you, but only just a little"
9. Iris blooming late
10. We're watching the days
11. Each one one in which
12. One kid doesn't die
13. Except the worlds of worlds that do
14. Faces in dreams under water

"I tried to prepare myself for what would be the worst day of my life. But when it came I was not prepared," says the father of one black boy shot in Florida. But his sobs on the radio do nothing to dissuade the 73% of Floridians who stand by stand-your-ground.

Says the senator: "Given the choice between a raped or beaten victim and a dead thug, I'll take the dead thug any day."

%

To kill the threat: A human right

Odysseus bends the bow and strings it. Telemachus stands at the ready. They have barred the exits from the house, preparing for slaughter.

%

In North Carolina 2,400 of those with permits to carry concealed weapons were convicted of felonies over a five-year period. 10 committed murder or manslaughter—8 with their guns.

Bobby Ray Bordeaux Jr. had a permit for a concealed handgun, despite a history of alcoholism, depression, and suicide attempts. Shot two men, killed one.

After convictions of rape, murder, and kidnapping, none lost their gun permits.

In North Carolina concealed weapons are allowed in public parks, soon in restaurants. Bit by bit we slide from "concealed" carry to "open."

%

The bullet made its way through the biker's helmet—his four-year-old son strapped into the bike seat. Maurice held a gun to his girlfriend's head in Asheville where the folk dancers make blackberry smoothies after church. (We have visited this territory before.)

Soon after Mr. Willis shot at his house with a rifle while his wife and daughter hid inside, he was released from prison and kept his permit.

Sgt. Lori Pierce, the "sole person" handling gun permits in her county: "I do not have time to conduct regular criminal checks on permit holders—too busy issuing permits," having granted 1,300 this year.

No permit required in Arizona, Idaho, Kansas, Maine, Mississippi, Missouri, New Hampshire, North Dakota, Vermont, West Virginia, or Wyoming (at this time).

Yesterday, My Historian stopped at my table. After we discussed the new gun rules at school, he stood still with nothing left to say. I was considering a sensation in my chest. I too had no further comments. On this topic, I was hysterical.

Allowing a sob would do just what?
I was afraid to look at my hands.

"He is wisest who knows, like Socrates, that his wisdom is worth nothing at all."

*

And now, having no one to receive these missives, I write into the space between atoms, the emptiness of organs lying dormant, all the aborted plans—

with my permit to carry a concealed weapon stapled to my eyeball

CHILD BIRTHDAY

Last wish: I yearn towards some philosophical song of truth that cherishes our daily life,

says Wordsworth, with which I entirely

concur

END THIRD MOVEMENT

FOURTH MOVEMENT:
ALL THAT IS SOLID

REAL LIFE REPORT

I miss something I have never had.

I long to return to a place I've never been.

I remember a hand that never once touched me.

TRY

Coleridge too noticed the through-line between think, thank, and tank

And Novalis: Language is a force-field of combinatory possibilities. Speaking only to speak we express the most stupid and original truths!

Start again: Only in free movement does the world render itself real

After B.L. constructed a room inside a room made entirely of salt, he led a goat into his house and watched him lick it to stubs and pools. The goat died, of course, of sodium poisoning and dehydration. B.L lay the goat's corpse on its side and cut a slit into its belly. Expecting the goat's entrails to fall through the slit, expecting the blood to pour, B.L. was shocked to discover nothing inside the goat at all—an empty carcass, and dry. He reached his hand into the cavern of the goat's torso, feeling for organs, something, and pulled out only a crystal, pure salt. B.L. now sliced the goat's body straight in half, and set one half on the floor, its empty and marvelous insides facing out. This he turned into a dollhouse for his daughter, then 4. Her dolls lived inside the goat, sitting on little chairs that B.L. fashioned out of shells glued to sticks. The dolls slept on beds made of abandoned hummingbird nests. There's some debate about what constitutes an installation as opposed to a sculpture. Certainly for B.L's little girl, the goat's body was "installation," though for her dolls it was only a hotel.

Wall gridded with nipples all ready to suck, some dripping. Another wall studded with nails the sharp way out: such contrasts made more palpable by scents of blooming lilies and milk spilled over the floor, the floor uneven, even rolling, so one slips on milk and steps on blooms and slides toward breasts or nails while gripping at ropes made only of light, a trick.

The first conversation between Telemachus and his mother is about art: Should the bard be allowed to sing his sad song?

Who is to blame for making us cry: the singer or the Gods who make things so sad?

*

As I told the grieving man, "When my mother got sick I thought to myself, *I will never be happy in the same way again.*"

"Was this true," he asked?

"Yes."

On the left side, a soft silt, a slip.

1. I determine to penetrate this strange longing
2. I am calm and stained
3. It flashes it prays it spreads
4. A lie on the lip of the day
5. The balloon in the wet grass remarks Evelyn
6. sits for a long time swaying or bobbing only slightly
7. Can you with your seven rats slow down?
8. And now the eyes gaze out from the wall
9. The orange flames of the body in the street
10. It suffers it matures it approaches
11. I cannot show beauty to you
12. I as old as I am am illusionary
13. Some come at last
14. Radio hour sun

In this room, there is nothing but a bed. There is no space to walk around it; to enter, you must climb on. It's a very comfortable bed, and so you lie down, rest your head on a pillow, pull the soft blanket up. Beside you is a man, twitching, even writhing, in pain. His breath is labored and occasionally he groans.

If you speak to him, he will not answer. If you try to touch him, he will flinch and move away. Lying there, you are on the one hand deeply comforted, and on the other, unbearably distraught.

"Real life takes on an almost exemplary quality"

Enormous projections of the inside of your own body. Heart and lungs on the right side, stomach, liver, kidneys on the left. The wall before you shows your brain, behind you, your womb and whatever might be inside it. If another person enters the room, the images will no longer be clear—for the inside of that person's body will be superimposed over yours. It will be difficult to tell whose lungs, whose heart, whose brain. Try breathing faster—see if you can discern the rhythm of your own lungs. But the other person might breathe faster as well. When a third person enters, then a fourth, the walls are a sea of light, color, moving forms. You wish the others would leave so that you could see yourself more clearly. But they are wishing this too.

Eyes are not focusing well. Nipples appear enlarged. Does the table "sway" toward me? I dream a garden full of flowers, though the petals fall (now I knew what to do with the poem).

Sex is the result but not always the motivation of turning toward the shoulder of the other. And is this swelling its effect? Believing where we cannot prove, zinnias bloom. Our little systems have their day. When blood flow increases in the veins of the breasts: a beam in darkness—let it grow. My girl watches me from across the room, pretty in a haircut.

*

"We can tell whether we are happy by the sound of the wind," I read. "It warns the unhappy man of the fragility of his house, hounding him from shallow sleep and violent dreams. To the happy man it is the song of his protectedness, its furious howling concedes that it has power over him no longer."

Happy/unhappy, I confront the racing heart while naming the underlying dead: one on the corner of 17th and Colorado, the other beneath a flat screen TV. Still others by the roadside, the doorway, the wayside.

As I consider their new formlessness, an anarchic breeze not kept out, I worry what forms within.

My freedom card bought a bit of an ad.
In California, the anarchists plan some property destruction
but the police are prepared.

And in the froth of not knowing what is up with the body, I manage my intake.
In the froth of not knowing what is up with the body, single out fallacies.

Write "backwards" into the night:

tnangerp eb thgim I

Or a: doolb fo lluf ylleb

*

Of the two options: "made poet" and "born poet" I'm a mourn poet.

Bidding a baby into the balanced family of capitalists—says Williams—(these orange
trees in blossom)—would create a tipping quickly righted.

As my cello playing child sleeps in, the anarchists are identified one by one.

A stone no longer supports its bridge.

INSTALLATION 11

Live birds glued to all four walls by their feet. A grid of birds from floor to ceiling, all around.

In the spaces between, bright circles of wet red paint (reapplied hourly). As the birds furiously flap, their wingtips dip and smear.

A moving red mass that cries.

(One begins by advertising oneself. One ends in madness.)

%

One cannot write, I then thought and said, without prison statistics in mind at all times: "the highest incarceration rate in the world, ahead of Turkmenistan, El Salvador, Cuba, Thailand and the Russian Federation."

And then, with such statistics in mind, do we write more or do we write less? Do we mention the cat tumbling down the stone stairs, or do we not? Do we include something called "play" or do we avoid it? These are the questions of real life. If the greatest, by which I mean largest, installation project called "What do you own? What owns you?" is underway right now all over the country, are we, we are, its makers.

One best friend's daughter needs her breathing tube expanded with a surgically implanted balloon. At eight her speech is blurred and she cries in her father's arms for a cookie. Another best friend's daughter asserts herself boldly in French. One best friend's daughter reenters the protest after tear gas clears. Another best friend's daughter cannot be found. Another's dies in infancy (when the yoga teacher played the song she died to, my friend walked out of class).

If I were to birth a fourth baby, odds would be against it. But this body in its red sweater was born for birthing others, even compromised others. Or so it most absolutely seems.

*

Inchoate aspects of the body announce themselves like leprechauns leaping from behind a tree.

The word "terminate." (But, little being, won't you terminate yourself?)

MELTS INTO AIR

I have yet to kill

> this seventh pregnancy, for I hope it will
> deliver itself up as blood and water

catching light

A PRO-LIFE INSTALLATION

Instead of a floor, a field of long grasses. Walls streaming water. Under the water, sheets of iron rust. You enter and lie down on the grass. Simulated sunlight headed straight for your belly hurts your eyes. But if you close your eyes, the ground will chill beneath you and the warmth from this "sun" will fade. You must keep your eyes open in order to stay warm. Yet the lulling sound of water, the heat below and above you, the blinding light, make it so hard.

You must "terminate" your stay.

%

If the candidate had his way, it would be illegal to end this pregnancy.
Whether or not I had a home. Whether or not a dime. Whether or not three children.
Whether or not I had time.

For the dirty world—feeling flexes.

Take a shower somewhere.

INSTALLATION 13

In which the body of the eleven-year-old girl, drowned off Long Island Sound, is
returned to her father. He lowers his hands from his face.

The room is not draped, lit, or in any way
                                    decorated.

At the gym, an old woman bends forward, naked to the world.
A man on the hill begins to feel the "vanity of his pursuits."

My country doesn't love women. It loves little girls far too much.

*

Must reason step in to control the excesses of raw nature?
A sword would make a precise slash: removing the "raw" fetus from the womb.

There is no limit that does not assume and resist the existence of the unlimited.
I want no god. The color red could do for the unbounded.

If what she desires is real life, she has to go all the way to death to get it.
Under the pink dress—an activated fantasy, excluded from the outside, but growing ·
within.

The disaster, if you want to go that far, is like the flapping or flipping weathervane
on top of a real house in real New England. How the shirts on the line bunch up
around the clothespins in that wind, trying to rip free.

The death of the fetus (baby, *thing*) will mark the birth of its parents, as a river
gives over to the sea.

The phenomenon of morning sickness is oriented around a determined lack, a valley.

*

A smear on the screen—it's always been there. I never wash it off. That's how I am.
Like some illicit sexual partner in a hotel, I'm sticking scraps of cloth into a plastic
bag: A kind of voluptuousness.

Blowing everything out of proportion for the sake of drama, trying to get all the way
from desire to disgust and back again, licking my lips in the museum where everyone
puts up with my smells, knowing how much money I have, knowing I could give it
all away at any moment.

1. How strange the mother's voice
2. Does the cat eat like a dog?
3. Everything tends toward the solid, the heavy
4. The vulgar
5. Dad laughs as though
6. The sway of these dead rhythms
7. Were one with his skin
8. I picture him alone
9. "To begin" "to lead" eventually "to rule"
10. This is my pouty response
11. A "philosophical" (systematic) approach to life
12. One can only attempt never achieve such an approach, following glimpses
13. This gift without a giver
14. My see-through belly

RED AGAIN

Today I wear red. And tomorrow.

Friends, Countrymen: I value most that which is neither swollen nor shrunken.
Father, Mother: I value most that which is neither yours nor yours.

Red for blood, for fire, for neon, and for Durga "the inaccessible."

*

> Wayward motes and falling water
> Tawdry tombs and laughing toddler
> Somber laundry calling daughter
> Dead pregnancy: There is no discernible
> order

But the question remains: whether to do it at home or in the clinic
Clinic: from klinikos: *of the bed*

1. In which the verb "to pull" gets special playtime.
2. In which I download *The Book of Embraces* only to find a pdf of 22,342 blank pages on my desktop
3. A chronicle of our early memories
4. of kissing one another
5. I knew a woman
6. seated under a window
7. who watched her baby die
8. The book of embraces
9. downloads next in Farsi
10. Dreamt a dog in a pool
11. There are can-do women and women who are just
12. done
13. I will give myself over
14. to the younger woman's hands

Hanging from invisible threads: a grid of swords. Points down, they sway slightly, glinting in the light. The tips of these swords dangle just above your head, or, if you are tall, might graze your crown. Shorter people, children, can walk unbothered. Tall women, most men, stoop or find their heads bloodied. Music: Dvořák cello concerto in B minor, practiced by a fourteen-year old, written in 1894, reluctantly and at the end of the composer's life. A tribute to his recently deceased sister.

OCTOBER 22

Looming trees and sturdy bureaus almost send me bedwards. I already vomited once every thirty minutes for seven hours (on the dot). The situation of living in a toxic world has delivered me. And still I must deliver the dead thing.

Panicked child at the door: I gave you everything I had. Work.

1. The spirit of

2. Malice survives

3. The direct exertion

4. Of malice. Give up

5. The desire to be female

6. The whatever-being

7. Defined not by what it is

8. And not by what it belongs to

9. But by belonging

10. Itself. The spirit of

11. Maleness survives the walking

12. Body. Give it

13. Over to be fucked

14. Into the non-state of being in common

1. My friend and I will take a walk: he is the best
2. Translator of poems
3. If ears are if open
4. Heart heats, threat retreats
5. I make a prayer in the form of a chart
6. A God in the form of a list
7. I have a funny little word sealed into a package
8. This living fat, diversity-street in real life, an eye brightly shining
9. And in the sweetness, piss
10. The clock ticks backward
11. Like a wasp at the bottom of the coffee cup
12. In all attempts to understand my own pettiness
13. I have made no progress
14. The archive is a radio soaked in senility

The thing was the size of a grain of rice, had no spine, but was very busy. Now not busy. Did it understand its own purpose? Though we told the Christian/psychologist/lawyer that we wouldn't be spending time saving the soul of a grain of rice, we did not say what we would be doing instead.

Is it a mandate now to serve some other god? After the stillbirth of his daughter, Dante Rossetti had this same question and named that god Beauty. Alice played Hera at the Greek fest. Her Hera made a peace offering to the attacking Egyptians. Her Hera made (or had Hephaestus make) a "gold box hooked with a beautiful emerald circular button." This gift the Egyptians dashed to the floor. However, once it hit the floor it began to glow so brightly that it burned the eyes of all the attackers (sparing the immortal gods), and this way the war was won.

In this story, you see, beauty wins the war, for beauty, the most desired thing, has a violence of its own. And so, while we did not say this to the Christian/psychologist/lawyer or to the kindly doctor or the bilingual nurse, or the receptionist who called me "Hon," we really did sacrifice a baby the size of a grain of rice for Beauty, though we'd give it another name, the name "Work" or the name "Peace."

Afterwards, the three living children climbed onto my bed, banging heads against one another in their haste to get closer to me. Forced to take turns in telling their days, they cried here and there, and the biggest one's limbs fell off the bed, so long, their glasses gleaming in the lamplight. The smallest sounded out her words.

The night before we scraped the grain of rice from my body, I'd dreamt of fields burning all around the few houses in which small groups of people huddled in fear.

The night after we scraped the grain of rice from my body I dreamt of a performance in which poets spoke poems that dissolved into only sound.

And in the morning, snow.

An outdoor installation. We install the tall doors outdoors. Thirty doors open out to the out. Thirty open in to the out. In all, sixty tall doors installed in the outdoors. Doors arranged in a range of angles, in a range of ways. Sway out sway in, doors in a wind. To be moved through and through again.

END FOURTH MOVEMENT

INTERLUDE: SILENCE IN 20 PIECES

1.

The boy handed me my change in the parking lot. It was precisely 9 hours after the killing. He saw my face.

"I hope you have a good rest of your day." No hope for the first part. It was five in the afternoon.

   Cloudy, windy, cold.

2.

It's difficult to move off the facts. Some are oblivious because they are demented or too young or because they too are dead. The frying bread in the pan. Exhaling hydrangea in their glass vase. Her little jacket rested on the back of her little chair.

Rests. I am allowed the present tense.

3.

Spent the weekend not telling children about the other children. At the birthday party, they made things out of clay. The youngest developed a fever, and the oldest learned to swing-dance. The curtains stood parted and I did not

close them. "I hope you're hanging in there," said one note.

4.

28 dead. 20 youngest
ones.

Is it "unspeakable"? She gets up

out of bed.

5.

May the circle be unbroken / by and by
lord by and

graves prepared, entered, complete. They will show us the faces of the murdered children, but not

       of their mothers and fathers.

6.

"Somewhere I am suddenly born."

And frantic at the paper. The burden is on you, flat map. If the president says the heart is outside the body, then the heart is outside the body.

Sisters at lunch: I read the transcript, says one. Don't read the transcript, I say. I did not dream in the night, but in the day when I was awake.

On this day, at this hour, in this place.

If the principal says we plan to live and learn joyfully,

then we plan to live and learn joyfully.

Map of the countryside with dormant fields under snow; human mouths have damaged the creeks.

A wind blows and bends the park slightly.

The dry air slides along.

7.

A line-graph reveals that gun owners are white with yanked back hair.

This is not the River Derwent. Not my nurse's song.

Running out of sugar, little mouse at the poison box?

I wanted to read something continuous and true. Gun ownership rates are inversely correlated with education. That, dear God, is continuous and true.

8.

Says the emergency room worker: Sometimes you enter into that room and you think
I can't do this again.

My colleagues around the world, she says, ask me what it is like to treat a gun wound,
since they've

        never seen one.

             I treat them every day, she says, speaking from
             Denver.

9.

    Mothers experience themselves as
    active. Until
    lobbyists
    press.

Kayne Robinson, Allan D. Cors, Chris W. Cox, Jim Porter, Chuck Norris, David
Keene, Wayne LaPierre, Peter Brownell, Oliver North, Dana Loesch: Look them up.

10.

And what are we to do with such nouns? Carry or throw or toss them? "Let's not talk about that," says Alice of the murdered children, "that is only silence." The windows of the school have bars. The policeman idles in his car out front. In his grim patience. "Up goes the smoke quietly as the dew exhales. We call that sadness."

11. [a film by Chick Strand]

Neon crucifix in slow spin. Carcasses on hooks for sale. You walk barefoot into six inches of silt. In the adjacent room, nothing but a puddle of water in which float 3 yellow rubber gloves.

12.

"You would think that the Connecticut government would be in support of our industry," pouts Mr. Chen, an executive from Colt Manufacturing Company.

Gun-maker

Men with gun cases stand in line at a pistol range.
Woman on her knees before the memorial for the children.
Allow me to be perfectly obvious. Allow me to be perfectly plain:

Colt employs 900 people in Connecticut. Ten-fold, twenty-fold, 100-fold are weeping at the memorials. At the threat of lost jobs, the state government quails.

13.

It's not an idle threat,

the industry rep explains.

One job:
Director of Government Regulations for the National Shooting Sports Foundation

14.

I wasn't going to speak, wasn't going to *establish myself*

    "Here where we / still live in a / real real / world"

but I did, I gave myself over to the devilish task: "to mourn in my complaint and make a noise."

15.

Those whispers just as you are falling —

    a snow-slick alley: I was in a frontal position
    at the screen

threading the self

threading the self into an alcoholic's blanket

16.

One month after those children are murdered, while others are falling all over the land, gun and ammunition sales soar and keep on soaring. Gun dealers say, "I've never seen such demand. If I had 1,000 AR-15s I could sell them in a week. When I close, they beat on the glass to be let in."

The phrase: *pervasive love*

17.

They were wearing grey, moving slowly. They were opening themselves again.

18.

I said the word "wound" in our little group of five, and the men's eyes went elsewhere, out the window. After that, their eyes did not come back. Out the window the sky was darkening, the temperature dropping, wind.

I said the word "wound" and the women looked up. I said, "There are two worlds, there really are," and no one disputed me, though perhaps we had different ideas about what or who made up these two worlds.

19.

There was a pool; we drained it to reveal the creatures at the bottom.
Massive eels slid out of our grip.

This is your defect, no one else's, it says.

20.

It was not death, not more death, I was after, though sometimes I imagined the blade
against my wrist as I fell into sleep. I was concerned with the gleam of icicles hanging
from the eves, with the smudge of blood on the underside of my girl's chin, with the
pair of underpants I found stuck between the bottom of the bed and the blankets.
Your jaw screwed into the mattress. Your back so hardly ever touched, so much like
snow falling in a whirlwind.

I was looking for a tighter press of bodies. And the sorrowful laughter of those who
discern the world shifting away.

FIFTH MOVEMENT:
Melts into Air

MERE

Spreading my legs like the poor redhead, I valued most of all
the chins of poets and their failures.

"The procreative truth of me petered out"

"Is our car tiny or huge?" asks Lucy. "What do you mean?" I say. "In the whole world, is our car tiny or huge?" "Tiny." "Are we tiny or huge, in the whole world?" "Tiny," I answer. "Or, huge."

*

Looked at from the perspective of her winsome gap-toothed—

there are so many gods.

*

"Real life is absent. We are not of this world."

Is your asshole private, public, or social?
[this line and its variances all around the book]

VULVIC EXPRESSIONS

We didn't anymore want inwardness. Our anger had become melodious, a form of overflowing, all the fluid in our bodies running into daylight. Our mouths and our vaginas were unable to shut, and so our leaders hated us, it was obvious. To each strand of our hair we attached our confessions. And yet the backs of our skulls, the souls of our feet remained sweetly and always hidden.

INSTALLATION 17

Low light. 17 prison beds screwed into each wall vertically, so that none can lie down. Mattress and bedding affixed to the frame, but there is gravity. Everything sags or pulls. In the center of the room: a hole.

Far down inside the hole, water gleams. Empty water glasses arranged in a circle around that hole, but no way to get the water out. Deeper than anyone's arm. Too narrow for a body.

Alternating blasts: strong and dusty wind / scent of ammonia.
The distance between our "moods" and their artificial proxies shrinks down.

The installation has no end. It therefore cannot be exited, nor can it be entered. However, it can be described: over and over again. Each time, a different set of components, a different composition, a new room.

The imagined installation presents the body as the last refuge.

It was a cagey evening.

In the novel, a man falls in love with a beautiful woman. For sixty pages, he pursues her with a single-minded focus: get to her body. When finally he takes off her clothes, he momentarily believes that she was "made" "for him"—her skin designed with his hands in mind, her legs completed when entwined with his own. Fucking her, he experiences himself as "whole," or more to the point, he experiences her as whole, made whole through his touch.

Then, just as he announces himself entirely happy, she tells him, "But I love my husband." Having staked his very life on having her, it now appears she belongs to another. His response, a few pages later, is to shoot her, from a rooftop, like a sniper. This was no doubt to be read allegorically, but it felt like real life.

On the night after I finished this novel, I sat up late with my daughter watching the senator in her white suit stand for 11 hours in a chamber of men who yawned, rubbed their faces, ate their take-out, looked away, and rolled their eyes while she, in her white suit, without water, without food, without sitting down, without leaning, without stopping once for the bathroom, spoke calmly, even sweetly, about women's bodies brutalized by pregnancy, about their lives, brutalized by children. She spoke on and on, not exhibiting pain, though pain she certainly experienced (her legs, back, feet, her jaw, eyes, tongue, belly). We imagined this pain while the men in their seats rubbed their eyes, ate their food, drank their coffee, and generally ignored her.

In the novel, the man cannot bring himself to shoot a dog, but he can shoot "beauty." The body of a woman is above all else, formal.

In the colo-

rado radio flash

the cop blogs his desire to eat women's
flesh.

I wrote the phrase: *intractable enigma*.

The soul is united only with itself.

*

Gorgeous one, wake me up: rescue me from the communitarian Hell that is my body.

Oh great — it's almost my birthday — the recalls underway — a public crisis —
among many —— we tried to look at the trees — but as soon as we came down the
mountain — it was just all sad again — I'm being pretty blunt — sometimes it's the
only way to be — I fell asleep early — cause love had abandoned me — my hair cut
short — was how I needed to be — I know — something — about love — you gotta
want it — bad — the boy played his cello and I would have indulged myself in crying
— but that I was holding — the video camera — trying to be steady — or blunt
— the Catholic senator was crying on the video — not the same video — crying for
the unborn — he really loved them —all the little babies — who are dying — even
right now — It's kind of weird — to love something — that doesn't actually exist
— except in the future — or maybe it's brilliant — magical and beautiful — to love
something that doesn't exist — except in the future — which is to say — in your
imagination - I can think about — babies too — how pretty they are — even when
they don't — exist — They are easier to love — than women who do exist — and
are yelling at you — or ignoring you — and are not beautiful — at all — "The sense
of touch makes nonsense — out of any dualistic understanding — of agency and
passivity" — says my philosopher — The legislator is crying — he's so full it falls
out of him — a "full" heart — no "anonymous dreaming stone" — crying is usually a
performance — if only for the self — like when kids stare into the mirror as they weep
— it's so fascinating to be a self that is so much a self — it dissolves itself — I kept
looking in the indexes — for the word "future" — and it wasn't there — so I settled
for — "installation" — and I found that word in the indexes — of all the books I
read — the "installation of pure reason" — the "installation of lighting" — the future
wasn't even mentioned by the philosopher of the future —

— was how I needed to be — I love the word "I" — and am against all forms of
embarrassment — that surround not just its use — but its nonuse too — I was given
this gift — it was, after all, my birthday — The narrative of failure — is as deep in

the family as the narrative of striving — one blurry patriarch — after another ——
though the women were funny — which was its own achievement — All my gifts —
sit around me like pets — the faces of the people — I admire the most — I can't seem
to distinguish — between admiring and loving — as a kind of steady state — just
felt and not genitally — in the bloodstream more generally — Breathing in a person's
presence — didn't really work — which was why I wrote — in my journal when I was
8 — a lot of times over — this was birth — on a bed with the window open — See
what it's like — if you really admire a person — and find their infancy — in their
aging face — you might want to destroy — all the things — that stand around — the
pavement the car the building — so that the person can float in a pure space — with
no obstructions — of course you can't do this — which is why you put them in the
poem — as a singular voice — there you are, super star —

AN IMAGE OF LOVE

Dad pulled the girl's hair into a ponytail and then suddenly, as if for the first time, we saw and adored her neck.

Even God is basically an aesthete.

Pulses of emotion / Ecstatic form

INSTALLATION: THE FUTURE

In the center of the room, a spacecraft designed only for probing—its long blue solar-panel wings, its insect-like body, at rest. Dozens of bats dart through the darkened room. On all four walls: the filmed history of the sun—from birth to death.

On loop.

1. And what was far is suddenly here
2. We woke to the crows, a sonic
3. saturation, a ruin
4. of isolation, as when on an airplane
5. the tray folds down
6. I woke hungry in the lines of my face
7. as if urban poetry with no real purpose
8. drifted down from the trees
9. It was spring
10. There were towers
11. glistening in a pool
12. with engorged moons
13. We woke to a sea
14. and the sounds of our sorrowing sons

INSTALLATION 24: A PUBLIC FOUNTAIN

A man in a veil. A red flower tattooed on his belly. An open wound on his forehead underneath the fluttering cloth. A bird hangs suspended beside him. Behind the man, whose eyes remain closed, rags of the sea. In his hand, a folded piece of paper. Take it from him, unfold it: written in cursive, the lyrics to "The Ballad of Easter Eve," which tells the story of three daughters sleeping while their mother writes letters to her murderer.

A FOURTEEN-LINE POEM ON MOTHERS

1. every day is full of figures
2. I abandon the city
3. in a dress you bought for me
4. a dog I once knew
5. is back resting in my lap
6. she's the cousin of nothing and
7. no one
8. the ankle just above the short sock on the boy
9. is a windswept token
10. of our desire
11. if men wear veils invisibly
12. if figs grapes olives and lemon cake
13. have I demanded more attention than I deserve?
14. oh, fox, my little fox

1. I have nothing to sell
2. I am the sign master
3. it inflates or fucks or loves
4. a spray of blood a luminous branch
5. the beginning is the negation
6. of the beginning
7. can you help me make my lunch?
8. and now the phone sits silent in my hand
9. the exaggerated beauty of the cello bow
10. it rattles it sinks it fingers
11. I was a child reading law
12. I wanted everyone to know I'd given my food away
13. some mothers leave their families
14. red chair white chair rug

Soon I will have to abandon this process. After all the work of mothering is done. Which is only soon to a planet.

"My mother was the daughter of a man from Lorraine."

"Kept pigs locked up in her closets."

"My mother was opposed to fasting and prayer."

"Drew and painted very well, until an accident left her all alone."

But first let me tell you one more tale:

> We ran and we ran and then we heard a sound. It was like a cannon going off. We thought it was a celebration, but when another went off too, we turned around and started to run the other way.

> There are those who are dead and those who are injured, and those who have lost their legs or feet.

> We had enemies. But we didn't know who they were, for we didn't know who we were. For me it was anyone on any side with a gun. But that wasn't enough. That wasn't really / clear enough.

*

And so we each chose our own enemies, since we did not know who the true enemy was.

What I thought was, what would justice look like in such a situation? And the answer came: *I am so sorry, no justice.* And then I thought, and was ashamed to think it, what's so important about the human?

The father saw his son on Facebook, his son with his two legs blown off. So that when a boy wrote a poem in which a girl's legs were only half visible, we were not sure if he meant her legs immersed in the healing waters of the sea or her legs ripped right from her body.

One by one the little victims recede to make space for new ones. Over and over:

"The lions in the lazy passages of time."

WHERE WERE YOU GOING WITH THAT?

Standing in line for our noodles, it occurred to me that if one of my children, say, shot someone at school, or say, planted a bomb at a marathon, I would no longer love that child. It would be easier than I'd previously thought to simply stop loving him or her.

Having no idea if that is true.

A FOURTEEN-LINE POEM ON ONCE HAVING BEEN A CHILD

1. I hate my desktop and my homepage
2. back when I was a child: three overlapping worlds
3. sequins on a windowsill
4. unrestrained futurism: like a hard cock with no conscience
5. I dreamed of a huge swimmer in the
6. alien air, dreamed
7. the clatter of emerald platters
8. in the whistle of a disco
9. serial cereals this and every
10. morning's marvel: my baby's been made
11. a man
12. there lies the melodious
13. rage of the garage
14. worker's wheels so slowly now

SYNTHETIC CRUDE

At least now I know the flavor of the universe—

They were breathless, they were giddy
at the spectacle of the State

Desire is its own work
writes my lonely friend

%

We are alone

says the 2017 UN report, in insisting that "while human rights are of fundamental
importance, they do not include rights that guard against dying of hunger, dying
from a lack of access to affordable healthcare, or growing up in a context of

total deprivation."

A concrete room, lit only from an open square cut into the ceiling: moonlight, sunlight, rain. Concrete floor, walls and ceiling: unadorned. In the center of the room, what could be a grave or a tub, filled with two inches of water.

Lying in this bed, bath, grave: a woman. She has nothing on; maybe she sleeps. Concrete backless chairs: one at her head, one at her feet, one on each side. The first strewn with sawdust, the next with hay, third with broken glass, the last with sewing needles. Each day a new order. Each day a new woman in the pool.

ANARCHIC BREEZE

A moment of inertia in which the writer gets stuck in a particular rhythm from which she cannot figure out how to escape

is a soft sift of self

*

Check my breasts for lumps while reading

the phrase: *swarm application*
the phrase: *shared drive*

        the body that is and is not mine

*

                                     (3 months
longer. Don't give up)

(I write this so that you will breathe and to prove that something was born)

Two brothers who always, throughout their childhoods, detested one another. Their parents learned that their only task, the only parenting skill they absolutely had to master, was to keep their sons apart. Of course the boys had separate rooms, separate schools, but they also needed separate mealtimes, separate vacations, separate outdoor play areas. As the boys grew older, the task of keeping them apart grew more urgent, for now they could do more harm to one another than simply cutting or bruising. Eventually, the doors between rooms were not enough. One boy or another would break a lock or shatter a door with his fists and feet, hard toys or tools, once, with an ax. The parents considered buying a separate house, keeping one boy in one with one parent, the other in the other with the other. But the parents loved each other; they had no wish to live apart. They loved the boys too, for as long as the boys were separated, as long as they were not aware of one another's presence, they were delightful. They enjoyed swimming, bike riding, coin collecting, and other harmless things, when alone. They read books, wrote stories, even sang songs to themselves, when alone.

The parents decided, finally, to build a wall in the center of the house, a brick wall with only one tiny door. This tiny door was made of steel, secured with heavy padlocks on both sides. These locks had only two keys; one hung from a chain around the mother's neck, the other around the Dad's. The parents passed back and forth through this door all day long, crawling on their hands and knees, and quickly locking the door behind them. No sound passed through the wall, and no light. And for a while, it worked. The brothers seemed to forget about one another. Each half of the house had its own door to the outside, its own family room, its own music. Inside their separate spaces, the brothers focused on their peaceful activities: stamp and coin collecting, reading, taking care of animals (one had a snake, the other, a rabbit). But then one day, as the mother was scurrying through the door with a sandwich for one son, the other son coughed. It was a tiny cough—more a clearing of the throat. It could have been a chair scraping the floor. It could have been a dog down the road. But the other brother knew; he'd recognize that cough anywhere. He stood to his full height (and he was quite big now, almost a man) and approached his mother, still on her knees. "What's there?" the brother asked, stepping toward the door. His mother, without thinking, clasped her hand to her chest—the key, under her shirt, between her breasts, its stillness, its perfect flatness. All art is entertaining on some level, entertaining a darkness, or a delight, entertaining a spirit or an arrogance, entertaining a rage.

*

And maybe you ask which brother is to blame? (Check our origins.)

1. I cannot freeze sound
2. or collapse phantom scaffolding
3. I open one contradiction after another
4. they call this "erotic intelligence"
5. or emptiness
6. where have you gone in your red dress?
7. your limbs only ever benign?
8. a soft belt of air
9. wraps or whips your waist
10. rose, iris, baby's breath, azalea
11. geranium, heliotrope, hydrangea
12. everything concerns the habitus and those who live there
13. so blow a generative swerve into remote tongues
14. softly interlocking

ANOTHER FOURTEEN-LINE POEM ON HEALING

1. they abused the powdery line
2. and collapsed the phantom scaffolding
3. on which we thought
4. we stood
5. where will you go now, you in your
6. red dress?
7. your benign limbs, at once
8. blessed and beautiful
9. naked as a word
10. you have done nothing wrong
11. and you are not condemned
12. the body's erotic intelligence
13. is all that there is
14. and is given

I wanted an installation that would figure violence without itself being violent. I wanted to see the body split without splitting a body. I wanted it to be "real." Why did I want this? I wanted to give my identity, my name, my family name, and my wallet in exchange for a purely liquid experience, but not one that I could never leave. Sometimes I wanted the opposite: to enter a room in which my body would become permanently marked (it was so already), in which other women would mark me. An owl mask, the peacock tail, the swollen ankles of the pilgrim. I wanted to place myself in a glass box and allow others to paint their pet names across the glass: *unassimilated; bluesy; complicit; poised; obscene; atrocity-warm-up.*

Then I realized I had not invented this fantasy, but had borrowed it from the male, so I obliterated the glass box and replaced it with a hole in the ground. This seemed the best display-case possible, a simple hole in the ground. But then there could be no viewer. A buried body is seen by no one.

This installation is called "Everybody wants some."

%

The installation artist wants to turn objects into performers
The installation artist wants to connect with people and build relationships
      like with a twin
She wants to respond to the space around her on a metaphysical level
The installation artist regards trauma and memory in a blue room with a low-hanging
      chandelier
He finances his art with a VISA card
Looks to anonymous urban spaces like bus shelters and phone booths
Makes a national monument out of human hair

INSTALLATION: TROPOS

      The horse is on the floor. The voice is turned hard. The word is smoke.
      The quiet woman burns. Horse-witch.

The earliest works were small and domestic—intimate theatrical settings no bigger than a child's bedroom. A man's coat hangs on a hook. A typewriter sits in a corner. Glass shards in a pile on a glass table. An opened diary difficult to read. The middle period is dominated by the outsized and absurd: huge lumpy beds, as if for giant trolls, grand pianos under spotlights, massive chandeliers spun of human hair threaded with teeth. Eventually these works outgrow the gallery, moving into the outer world. At the apex of this middle period, we have a work that spreads across a desert (an arrangement of stones best viewed from the air) and another that extends the entire length of the Colorado River (a silk ribbon that seems never to end). But the third period returns, bit by bit, to the intimacy of the first, drawing our attention once again inward. First the dirt and rocks of the landscape find their way back into the gallery: piles of stones, circles of sand, trees and grasses growing right from the floor. Next the weather itself moves indoors: fine mists, rainbows, artificial sunlight, or the total darkness of night. Now that what was "outside" is "in," human forms are reintroduced—the body itself, its basic functions (eating, sleeping, sex), its extravagant acts (dance, acrobatics)—and then the orifices become installations all on their own: insects crawl from the woman's vagina, Jell-O spills from her mouth. As the focus of the installation goes further inward still, by way of technology's ever more probing devices, it reaches the very organs, nervous systems, and hormones of the body: imaged, charted, graphed.

What explains this movement, this swelling and contracting?

A FOURTEEN-LINE POEM ON GIVING UP

1. to kiss the woman in her grey dress

2. a sharp rise, an extravagant claim

3. the first words are words of want

4. something that is in us and that surpasses us

5. I leaned a book against the door

6. unlocked the car from a distance

7. pulled clover from the grass

8. the wind is no gender

9. the negation of troubled desire

10. is like a stamp I lick that won't stick

11. phantom on the roof

12. in the form of a moss

13. grows thick

14. dear J.

After the philosophers gathered in the park under a heavy cloud. After the children ran to the trees waving sticks and then hid. After teens sulked. After flags. After the city changed. After tender grass tips. After standing on our hands. Beautiful cloudy girl bikes by. Aged man with camera shoots the grill. We depart from all that is reasonable. After the lips rubbing. After the gravestones and the unmarked graves. After they forced the women to walk among the exhumed bodies of the dead. After she walked among the bodies of the children beginning to rot. After her own children became noxious to her. Ships, timber icy, waiting in the bay. After sunrise the sailors approached the shore. Slept on sand with bellies exposed, rivulets of blood. After blood. After the German health worker devoured her steak. After six weeks in Mexico City and six further weeks in Colombia. After the dictators. The smoker hunched. The boy played war until the girl came and then they ran. Flowers teddy bears balloons and flags, after cookies. After I loved you curled in my lap, the flowing cup, rivers windhovers shore birds and I was exhausted nearly asleep: we had to begin again.

A FOURTEEN-LINE POEM ON NOT GIVING UP

1. a freckle between her shoulder blades
2. I keep trying to zip it
3. I have never
4. this system of marks, scrapes and wounds
5. on stage or screen or page
6. made clear
7. no no
8. but I wanted to be some kind of healer or farmer
9. or else to be the wounded one
10. to make my mother cry
11. desire achieves its lastingness
12. pity narrative
13. the body the
14. astringent bright blooms

*

I commit to stay committed until the very end.

This installation is on the outside of a building, rather than within. The walls are brick. To enter, go out and look up. Seven bodies suspended from ropes hang at various heights. The ropes, from old fishing ships, wrap around their waists, chests, or hips. The bodies are naked and their torsos have been cut, one could say, "flayed" (this could be an effect of makeup, or the wounds could be real). They hang, more or less horizontally, with limbs dangling. Eyes are closed. Faces hard to read. Silences, they just sway. Almost imperceptibly they are lowering. The installation is called "Resurrection."

Viewers might seat themselves in chairs set randomly around. When it begins to rain the viewers will rise. Not water but seeds are falling—on the viewers and on the bodies that sway.

A FOURTEEN-LINE POEM ON RESURRECTION

1. "when will I see you again?"
2. at the edge of the window: a crimson streak of sun
3. I tend our "prison guard" with daily eyes
4. say everything simply
5. or build me a city
6. of only terms I have to look up
7. to see the way the moon fills so
8. erotically a Lucy
9. but I didn't find you in June and I didn't
10. find you in July. Pink
11. stones shiny stones
12. American red dust
13. blood dust
14. rising

EVERYBODY WANTS SOME

"The world is evil and we don't need to grieve for it," says the woman on the academic conference panel.

(So why do we so want our children to desire it?)

ONCE ONLY AGAIN AND AGAIN

Once only again and again: imagine the morsel, if possible, of Jewish resistance—
the charred chair, no windows, more morbid far arrests, the red and the black, the
unburied. Once and once again once, a woman comes through the door, pushing her
hair back from her face, a hedonistic moment, like poetry night in Glasgow, or like a
seaside town where teenagers film themselves reading from notebooks while sitting
on statues in the winter. Imagine, if you can, their flowing flower-eyes, so that you
might once and once again address the State with a little mouth full of water.

1. sway fervently
2. that witch teaches corners to be corners
3. it is not necessary to apologize
4. for Ignorance incapable of Concealing itself
5. pleasure scares us
6. in time with this endless speaking
7. in time
8. with clouds set to drift
9. humility assumes a relationship to nothing
10. since just to be is no achievement
11. I didn't want to write a thesis: walnuts fall from the tree
12. didn't want our pluralism to keep reducing to a unity
13. so I make my way toward you
14. fervently

%

Writing, finally "To be a universe! To be a universe!" This was "writing by a God in whose hand the breath was."

AGAIN LIFE

And girls with jewely glances, anarchists cooking spaghetti for gamblers, women giving birth in tandem while holding hands: *open, yeasty, limitless, permissive!*

A FOURTEEN-LINE POEM ON THE END OF THIS

1. I am
2. very hungry
3. but not a
4. cruel ruler or an idle
5. fool I am
6. content not to be
7. read or pressed
8. into service I serve
9. anyway in an enclosure
10. falsely made
11. believed in only momentarily
12. abandoned for an opening
13. that itself closes I
14. un-repent

As the light bulbs burn out, one by one, as the dark sky stays dark into morning, as the pretty children sleep, as the surveillance machine balloons, as I soften the earth, as I get subjectivity all wrong, as I care about feeling and then apologize for caring, as I monitor the sunflower, as I acquire near resentments and new fears, as I dream of the chicken carcass rotting in the airport bathroom, as I accept my own resignation, as I remember my father and my mother, as I am riveted to Howard Zinn, as I banish various thoughts, as I banish them in order to sleep, as I then coax the thoughts back through dreams and try to recall them on waking, as I kiss the five-year-old face, as I hold my husband's balls, as I consider with the philosophers the problem of the other, as I feel myself apart and together at once, "an otherness barely touched upon that already moves away," as I structure an insolent happiness, as I join a revolution that doesn't exist, as I breathe my body, as I plan the menu, as I extend nerves through air, as I think through a letter I will never write, as I give myself over to the letter I will not write, as I what the fuck Ohio, as I perform the transcript of the filibuster, as I consent to contact, as I peer at the replica of the city as it once was, as I sit on the concrete bench gazing on the concrete wall, as I turn my head to breathe, as I am a stranger to my mother, I slip from Real Life again.

ANOTHER FOURTEEN-LINE POEM ON THE END

1. I am a

2. sorry

3. and often

4. stupefied

5. citizen I have stolen

6. so many languages where

7. does my body end

8. hooked rather abruptly

9. by my friend

10. into a collective orientation

11. toward the knowledge-object as future

12. project I pursue

13. the gap

14. between what I want and what I know

1. Aimé Césaire saw the ocean as a great vociferous mouth eating the beach
2. Description fails as girls scramble skyward on stones
3. Empire is a style
4. Of revolutionary terrorism
5. And I am beholden to
6. A god made of
7. Glass and a doctor called Doctor of
8. Hands or The Doctor of Hands
9. To whom all creatures owe their birth
10. I air
11. Was Julie or Julia or Jula or
12. Jewel
13. A doctor called "Work" or "King" or
14. "Killing"

Live mammals—a goat, a cow, a dog, a wild boar—suspended from the very high ceiling of the nave of a church. They bark, moan, squeal, and bellow. Strapped into harnesses, legs down. Of course they shit. Animal shit on the floor of this "church." You enter and stare up (neck straining), try to dodge the shit. You can't dodge shit that's at your feet and head at once. The animals' legs run frantically in the air. Muted light, holy light, falls through the long high windows with their stains.

PUBLIC SERVICE

The translation of Spinoza goes: "when God is considered as a thinking being" or "when God is considered as a being who acts." Provisional. About as illusive as language (as allusive too), God perpetrates itself in this public service announcement.

THE CUT

Perhaps this is what I've been doing all along: stashing my rage in a mother's laugh

%

The eagle   slashes

shadows of bags

                         The only arena of longing

is this

%

Some Gods are chronically against all writing

but I know no better way to exceed my vision

THE HUMBLE VIEW

And so I tried to make my writing inseparable from life

A sonic exercise—putting my mouth on your ear

*

The lyric was like a box a child crawls into

*

Or it was like the sun run round
with all that we had found
to have loved

END

Sources in order of first appearance

John Ashbery, Chris Nealon, Chad Kautzer, Robert Duncan, Andrew Zawacki, Adrienne Rich, Paul Krugman, Lyn Hejinian, Carl Andre, Fred Moten, Marcel Duchamp, Ulises Carrión, Serena Chopra, Giorgio de Chirico, James Baldwin, César Vallejo, Jacques Rancière, Fyodor Dostoyevsky, Charles Olson, Guillaume Apollinaire, Jennifer Doyle, Gertrude Stein, Charles Blow, Kurt Schwitters, William Shakespeare, Thomas Hardy, Patrick Greaney, James Brown, Joseph Karl Radler, Damien Hirst, Roberto Tejada, Antonio Gramsci, Alice Notley, Carsten Holler, Claire Bishop, Félix González-Torres, Joseph Beuys, Stéphane Mallarme, Plato, William Wordsworth, Novalis, Evelyn Reilly, Janet Cardiff, Theodor Adorno, Inger Christensen, Lisa Robertson, Psalm 55, Mina Loy, André Breton, Judith Butler, Pierre Hadot, *Melancholia*, Sara Ahmed, Fred Moten and Stephano Harney, Walter Benjamin, Spinoza. For a more detailed list of source texts, see www.omnidawn.com/sources-real-life.

Acknowledgments

Gratitude to the editors of the following publications in which pages from *Real Life: An Installation* appeared, often in earlier drafts:

The Academy of American Poets Poem-a-Day, *The Baffler*, *The Best American Poetry 2015*, *The Colorado Review*, *The Elephants*, *Essay Press Chapbook Series*, *Fence*, *Kenyon Review*, *Laurel Review*, *Liberation: New Works on Freedom from Internationally Renowned Poets*, *Make Literary Magazine*, *The New Republic*, *Oversound*, *Pinwheel*, *Public Pool*, *Spoke Too Soon*, *Touch the Donkey*, *Under a Warm Green Linden*, *Verse*, *Volt*.

Thank you to beloved friends for reading and for listening to me talk about this book over the years and for inspiring its making, especially K.J. Holmes, Chad Kautzer, Fred Moten, Linda Norton, Lisa Olstein, Jennifer Pap, Jeffrey

Pethybridge, John-Michael Rivera, Margaret Ronda, Selah Saterstrom, Mathias Svalina, and Andrew Zawacki. Thank you to listeners at many readings who have encouraged and energized me. Thank you to Benjamin, Alice, and Lucy for the language, and for my real, real life. Thank you to Rusty Morrison, Trisha Peck, Cassandra Smith and the whole Omnidawn crew for continued faith and support.

The installations described in this book, along with others, can be found on the website www.reallifeaninstallation.com. Thank you to the artists who have created these realizations: Sam Ace, Abraham Avnisan, Colleen Barry / Mount Analogue, Nina Berfelde, Amaranth Borsuk, Serena Chopra, Brent Cox, Michelle Ellsworth, Erin Espelie, Yanara Friedland, David Gatten, Amir George, Miguel Gutierrez, Féi Hernandez, K.J. Holmes, Benjamin M. Johnson, Anansi Knowbody, Jeanne Liotta, Leah Lovett, J. Michael Martinez, Gesel Mason, Linda Norton, Jeffrey Pethybridge, Luther Price, Benjamin Roberts, Carin Rodenborn, Selah Saterstrom, Jennifer Scappettone, Kelly Sears, Ximena Serrano, Robert Sniderman, Joe Steele, Joel Swanson, Edwin Torres, Niki Tulk, Danielle Vogel, Phuong Vuong, Andrew Zawacki and others.

An enormous thank you to Phuong Vuong for creating the Real Life website and to Mona Hatoum for her generosity in allowing us to feature her work on the cover of the book and the website.

And thank you to Tim Roberts for sparking the idea for this book and, as always, for most miraculous love.

photo by Laird Hunt

Julie Carr lives in Denver. This is her tenth book.

Real Life: An Installation
by Julie Carr

Cover art:
Mona Hatoum, *Suspended*, 2011
High pressure laminate and metal chains
Dimensions variable
© Mona Hatoum. Courtesy White Cube (Photo: Hugo Glendinning)

Cover typeface: Avenir LT Std, Garamond 3 LT Std
Interior typeface: Copperplate Gothis Std, Garamond 3 LT Std

Cover & interior design by Cassandra Smith

Offset printed in the United States
by Thomson-Shore, Dexter, Michigan
On 55# Enviro Natural 100% Recycled 100% PCW
Acid Free Archival Quality FSC Certified Paper

Publication of this book was made possible in part by gifts from:
Mary Mackey
Francesca Bell
Katherine & John Gravendyk, in honor of Hillary Gravendyk
The Clorox Company
The New Place Fund

Omnidawn Publishing
Oakland, California
Staff and Volunteers, Fall 2018

Rusty Morrison & Ken Keegan, senior editors & co-publishers
Gillian Olivia Blythe Hamel, senior poetry editor & editor, *OmniVerse*
Trisha Peck, managing editor & program director
Cassandra Smith, poetry editor & book designer
Sharon Zetter, poetry editor, book designer & development officer
Liza Flum, poetry editor
Avren Keating, poetry editor & fiction editor
Anna Morrison, marketing assistant
Juliana Paslay, fiction editor
Gail Aronson, fiction editor
SD Sumner, copyeditor
Emily Alexander, marketing assistant
Terry A. Taplin, marketing assistant
Matthew Bowie, marketing assistant
Mia Raquel, marketing assistant

Only a poet can humble us to the gunshot ghost of the America behind its dream. Julie Carr's resonant genius is at our ears; just look at what's in your hands now, open it, read it. You will join me in saying, Oh Yes, you have made poetry inseparable from life, thank you for showing us the courage to keep them together. We need this poetry.

CAConrad, author of *While Standing in Line for Death*

Ordinary life is anything but ordinary. In its daily rhythms a million universes enact themselves in all directions. In *Real Life*, Julie Carr builds out of essay, poem and fragment this chronicle of infinite dailiness full of what Jean Valentine called "this-world." As we negotiate and are mediated by multiple languages— intimate, commercial, informational, political—the text runs in simultaneous modes that delineate the condition of the modern mind. Fairy tales meet financial facts. Somehow in the narrative of sociality we try to remain human.

Kazim Ali, author of *Inquisition*

Julie Carr's *Real Life: An Installation* is a breathtaking feat of imagination, intellect, and empathy. As she writes, "I want to make something from nothing, to fill the empty vault of a national cry" and this book fulfills that cry. *Real Life* is a lapidary mourning song in this age of precarity; a durational epic that exquisitely logs the layered realities that overwhelm and impair us from acting. Carr finds threads of truths in not only the statistics of gun deaths but in the worlds that her children and artists create as both a space from and against state violence. Throughout, Carr questions how to make real this state violence dematerialized by late capital; how to "figure violence without itself being violent." *Real Life* is an impressive poetics of possibilities; her sonnets and imagined installations are blueprints of art-making that disturb, move, and awaken us.

Cathy Park Hong, author of *Engine Empire: Poems*